THE X FILES

UNCOVERING GREASTEST MYSTERIES

By Saahil

Preface

For over a decade, I embarked on a journey through time and space, into the realms of the unknown and the enigmatic. The pursuit of answers, the thirst for knowledge, and an unyielding curiosity led me on a quest to explore some of the world's most perplexing and captivating mysteries. From vanished flights to ancient civilizations, from supernatural occurrences to historical riddles, this book is the culmination of more than eleven years of tireless research, investigation, and the unending pursuit of truth.

In these pages, I strive to unveil that truth, or at the very least, to shed light on the shroud of mystery that has surrounded these enigmas for generations. Each chapter takes you on a gripping journey, uncovering the stories, facts, and theories that have left countless individuals baffled and intrigued.

From the depths of the ocean to the vastness of the cosmos, from the untamed wilderness to the corridors of ancient civilizations, this book aims to captivate your imagination, challenge your understanding of reality, and spark the flames of curiosity. It invites you to peer into the abyss and contemplate the unexplainable, the supernatural, and the extraordinary.

While not every chapter may offer a concrete answer, each one provides an opportunity to explore the enigmatic, the bizarre, and the unknown. So, open these pages, embrace the unknown, and join me on a journey that will take you from the depths of the Earth to the outer reaches of the universe, uncovering the greatest mysteries that have long intrigued humanity.

Dive in, and let the quest for answers begin.

Saahil

Contents

1. Vanishing Act: Airlines Flight MH370

On the 8th of March, 2014, at precisely 12:42 AM, a Malaysian Airlines flight MH370 took off from Kuala Lumpur International Airport. This routine flight was bound for Beijing, China, carrying 227 passengers, 10 flight attendants, and two experienced pilots: Captain Zaharie Ahmad Shah, a 53-year-old veteran, and First Officer Fariq Hamid, a 27-year-old on a training flight. Captain Zaharie, a senior pilot with extensive experience, was at the helm of this Boeing 777 aircraft.

For the initial 20 minutes of the flight, everything proceeded as usual. At 1:08 AM, the plane crossed over the Malaysian coastline, entering the airspace above the South China Sea, heading towards Vietnam. Captain Zaharie reported that the aircraft was cruising at 35,000 feet, and all systems appeared normal. However, approximately 11 minutes later, as MH370 entered Vietnamese airspace, the unexpected occurred.

Kuala Lumpur's Air Traffic Control radioed the plane, saying, "Malaysian 370, contact Ho Chi Minh. 120.9. Goodnight." In response, Captain Zaharie replied with a simple, "Good night. MAS 370." Those were the last words ever heard from the flight.

Soon after, Malaysian Airlines Flight MH370 inexplicably vanished from radar screens, marking the beginning of one of the most perplexing mysteries in aviation history.

The disappearance of MH370 unfolded within 30 seconds after entering Vietnamese airspace, vanishing from radar screens at 1:21 AM. At this point, Kuala Lumpur's Air Traffic Control initially did not notice the disappearance and assumed that the plane had flown out of radar range and into Vietnam's airspace. Similarly, the Vietnamese Air Traffic Control spotted MH370 entering their airspace but then watched as it suddenly vanished from their radar screens. They tried to establish communication with the aircraft, but there was no response. After 18 minutes of fruitless attempts, Vietnamese controllers alerted Kuala Lumpur that MH370 had disappeared without a trace.

In standard procedure, Kuala Lumpur's Aeronautical Rescue Coordination Centre should have been alerted within one hour of the plane's disappearance. Unfortunately, it took nearly four hours to initiate an emergency response. By 6:32 AM, the time when MH370 was supposed to land in Beijing, a massive search operation was launched to locate the missing aircraft.

Given its flight path, the initial search efforts concentrated on the South China Sea, an area encompassing the maritime boundary between Malaysia and Vietnam. This search quickly escalated into an international effort involving 34 ships and 28 aircraft from seven different countries. Yet, despite these extensive efforts, the plane remained elusive, and no trace was found.

Approximately four days after the plane's disappearance, on the 12th of March, it was reported that a military radar had detected the aircraft, even though civilian radar had lost track of it. According to this military radar data, the last sighting of MH370 occurred at 2:22 AM. Notably, the plane was no longer above the South China Sea. Instead, it had shifted westward from Malaysia, above the Strait of Malacca and headed toward the Andaman and Nicobar Islands.

This revelation was nothing short of astonishing, as it contradicted the expected flight path towards Beijing. Instead, it appeared as though MH370 had reversed course and was now flying south, away from its intended destination.

This development left the world bewildered, raising numerous questions. Where was the plane heading now? Could it have veered toward India, perhaps even crashing in the Himalayas or Kazakhstan?

A few days later, investigators unearthed a crucial piece of evidence from satellite data. MH370 had made attempts to automatically establish communication with a satellite, a not uncommon occurrence for large aircraft like the Boeing 777. This was akin to your smartphone attempting to connect to known Wi-Fi networks automatically.

However, the satellite communications raised further questions. While the plane had made contact with the satellite, it had done so without transmitting any information about its precise location. The satellite merely confirmed that MH370 had initiated contact, but it revealed nothing regarding the aircraft's whereabouts.

Intriguingly, scientists and investigators endeavored to exploit this satellite communication to approximate the plane's location. Their logic was that when MH370 contacted the satellite, the satellite would have repositioned its antenna in the direction of the aircraft. Armed with this knowledge, they utilized the angle of the satellite's antenna to make calculations, ultimately estimating a region within which the plane might be located.

The exact coordinates of MH370 could not be pinpointed through satellite data alone, but they were able to determine that the aircraft was somewhere within a broad circle. Each instance of attempted communication with the satellite was represented by a white circle. In this case, seven white circles, known as Satellite Handshakes, depicted the times at which the plane contacted the satellite. The last circle represented the most recent point of contact with the satellite, indicating the aircraft's potential location.

The extent of the uncertainty was staggering, as the final circle encompassed a vast expanse of territory. The plane might be located anywhere within this circle, which stretched from Kazakhstan, China, and Indonesia to Australia, covering a substantial portion of the Indian Ocean.

The aircraft attempted to communicate with the satellite seven times, hence the presence of seven white circles. With each new circle, they moved closer in time to the moment of disappearance. The final, seventh circle illustrated the last instance of attempted communication, marking the aircraft's potential whereabouts before losing contact. To narrow down the possibilities, investigators embarked on a complex series of calculations.

These calculations considered factors such as the plane's speed, its remaining fuel, and the time at which contact ceased. Ultimately, they estimated a particular region within the vast circle as the most likely location. This area on the arc became known as the "7th Arc." It was situated approximately 2,000 kilometers west of Australia and covered a substantial area of the Indian Ocean. This location was uncharted territory, relatively unexplored and uncharted in terms of its oceanic geography.

Subsequently, numerous search operations were launched to explore the potential resting place of MH370. Yellow shaded regions on maps indicated areas where these searches were conducted, and the orange area highlighted the priority search region, where the most extensive efforts were concentrated.

By April 2014, surface search operations were discontinued. The expectation that the aircraft would remain afloat on the ocean's surface was dashed. The prevailing theory suggested that if MH370 had indeed crashed, it would have sunk into the depths of the ocean.

The search continued, with deep-sea exploration taking center stage. This marked the largest and most costly search operation undertaken thus far. Over weeks, months, and eventually years, they scoured the ocean floor in search of the elusive plane. Regrettably, their efforts proved fruitless. In 2017, three years after the plane's disappearance and following the expenditure of $160 million, the search was officially terminated, marked by its inability to locate the aircraft.

However, amidst the ongoing search efforts, a glimmer of hope emerged in July 2015. The first piece of debris from MH370 was discovered. This fragment had journeyed across the ocean, eventually reaching Réunion Island, located east of Madagascar in the Indian Ocean. The identified debris was a flaperon from the plane, a broken segment serving as a critical clue.

In 2018, an American company, Ocean Infinity, struck an agreement with the Malaysian government to initiate a new search operation. Their contract offered a "no find, no fee" arrangement. With advanced underwater surveillance equipment at their disposal, Ocean Infinity embarked on a new search mission. In addition to searching for the plane, they conducted detailed underwater mapping, unveiling a complex ocean floor terrain.

During this operation, their investigations uncovered underwater volcanoes, cliffs, and mountainous features beneath the surface of the ocean. The operation lasted for several months, during which they conducted extensive surveys. However, despite their advanced technology and meticulous searches, they too were unable to locate the missing aircraft.

Faced with continued frustration in the search efforts, attention turned to the backgrounds of the plane's passengers and crew, and a closer scrutiny of the pilots' history. Investigators explored potential scenarios, including the possibility of hijacking or pilot involvement in the plane's disappearance.

From these inquiries emerged several theories regarding the fate of MH370. Each theory attempted to shed light on what might have transpired on that ill-fated flight. Let's delve into these theories one by one.

Theories and Assumptions

1. Captain Zaharie Shah's Involvement: The first theory implicated Captain Zaharie Shah, suggesting that he intentionally disabled communication systems, commandeered the aircraft, and deliberately crashed it into the ocean. But what could have motivated such actions? Speculation ranged from mental health issues to suicidal

tendencies and even potential motives related to hijacking or terrorism.

- Supporting Arguments for Shah's Involvement: Advocates of this theory pointed to specific elements of the flight path. Notably, the aircraft executed a nearly 180-degree turn back toward Malaysia, a maneuver believed to be executed manually. Additionally, MH370 flew directly over the border between Thailand and Malaysia, implying a deliberate attempt to avoid the radar systems of both countries. A noteworthy factor was the presence of a flight simulator at Captain Zaharie's home, which contained a path resembling MH370's flight path, sparking suspicion.

- Countering Arguments: Those who refuted this theory highlighted Captain Zaharie's impeccable record as a highly experienced pilot and respected figure within the airline. No evidence suggested personal or financial troubles that might have led to such actions, and investigators failed to uncover any behavioral red flags or motives for his involvement in the plane's disappearance.

2. Hijacking and Terrorism: A second theory suggested that hijackers or terrorists might have been responsible for MH370's fate. This theory gained traction when two Iranian passengers with stolen passports were identified. These passengers had initially taken a flight to Beijing with the intent of continuing on to Europe.

- Suspect Passengers: The presence of these Iranian passengers with stolen passports raised suspicion. However, further investigations indicated that their intention was likely not terrorism but rather an attempt to relocate to Europe using fraudulent identification.

- Interpol Confirmation: Interpol lent support to this theory, asserting that the individuals in question were unlikely to be terrorists, strengthening the case against hijacking or terrorism.

3. Oxygen Deficiency: The third and perhaps most plausible theory posits that oxygen deficiency led to the incapacitation of passengers and crew, including the pilots. This theory suggests that the entire plane lost consciousness, leaving the aircraft to operate on autopilot until its fuel was exhausted, ultimately resulting in a crash into the ocean.

- Possible Scenarios for Oxygen Depletion: This theory encompasses various possibilities, such as an electrical fire in the cockpit, a catastrophic technical failure, or a sudden accident that resulted in a rapid loss of cabin pressure.

- Supporting Evidence: The theory gains credibility through the observation of several facts. Notably, the aircraft executed a sharp turn, reversing course over the border between Thailand and Malaysia. This maneuver could indicate an attempt to escape both countries' radar systems.

- Countering Arguments: Critics of this theory point out that a seasoned pilot like Captain Zaharie would not engage in such actions without a compelling reason. Moreover, the absence of a distress signal or a clear explanation for the plane's sudden deviation from its intended flight path raises questions.

While these three theories represent the most widely discussed scenarios regarding MH370's disappearance, it is important to acknowledge that numerous other theories and speculations have surfaced throughout the years. These have ranged from far-fetched ideas about alien abduction to allegations of military involvement, all of which lack substantial evidence and remain on the fringes of credibility.

As of 2022, a significant breakthrough emerged in the quest to locate MH370. Richard Godfrey, a retired aerospace engineer, introduced a novel approach to solving the mystery. He employed radio wave technologies, drawing data from the British Inmarsat Satellite, Boeing, Australian oceanographers, and WSPRnet, an amateur radio wave technology network. His methodology combined elements of data analysis and oceanographic research to determine the potential location of the aircraft.

Through this intricate approach, Richard Godfrey harnessed radio wave reflections to trace MH370's probable path. This innovative technology relies on the reflection of radio waves in the atmosphere to detect aircraft flight paths. Essentially, when an aircraft interferes with these radio waves, it becomes detectable.

Godfrey developed a computer program capable of identifying flight paths through these weak signals. Utilizing the knowledge that MH370's disappearance correlated with the reflection of these radio waves, he was able to compute its potential location.

In his analysis, Richard Godfrey asserted that MH370 rests precisely on the 7th Arc, approximately 4 kilometers beneath the ocean's surface. This location aligns with the theory that the plane eventually descended into the southern Indian Ocean.

While his approach was met with some skepticism, Godfrey's methodology, if accurate, could provide a clear breakthrough in the search for MH370. His calculations are precise, with an accuracy of approximately 40 nautical miles for the plane's underwater location.

Richard Godfrey advocates for a new search operation within a 40-nautical-mile radius of this calculated point, expressing confidence that this focused effort may yield the long-sought discovery. Importantly, this area is significantly smaller than those previously explored during search operations.

To validate his claims, Richard Godfrey conducted a drift analysis to examine the ocean's currents. The objective was to determine whether the ocean currents could have carried debris from the plane to various locations, thereby correlating with the newfound underwater location. Notably, 27 pieces of debris from MH370 have been discovered on various islands across the world, which aligns with the drift analysis.

The quest to locate Malaysian Airlines Flight MH370 has spanned nearly a decade, marked by numerous search operations, theories, and investigations. The disappearance of this aircraft has baffled the world and haunted the families of the 239 people onboard.

However, the recent breakthrough introduced by Richard Godfrey and the alignment of the drift analysis offer a promising glimmer of hope. If his calculations prove accurate, and a new search operation within the 40-nautical-mile radius yields results, the mystery of MH370's disappearance may finally find resolution.

As we await further developments in this ongoing saga, the desire for answers endures. The fate of MH370 remains one of the most enigmatic aviation mysteries in history, and its ultimate discovery would provide closure to the families of those who were on board, as well as bring clarity to the aviation community.

In the absence of definitive proof, the mystery of Malaysian Airlines Flight MH370 continues to intrigue, captivate, and challenge our understanding of modern air travel and the depths of the oceans that conceal its secrets. The dedication and persistence of investigators, scientists, and researchers fuel the hope that this enduring puzzle will one day be solved.

2. Tragedy in the Skies: The China Boeing 737 Plane Crash

On the 21st of March 2022, a seemingly routine day for air travel, Flight MU-5735 prepared for departure from Kunming, China. The clock displayed 1:11 PM, and passengers, likely unaware of the impending tragedy, boarded the aircraft with a mix of anticipation and normalcy. The flight was a typical two-hour journey, taking passengers to Guangzhou, a bustling city situated in Southeast China.

As Flight MU-5735 taxied down the runway and lifted into the sky, it mirrored countless other passenger flights that had embarked on similar routes. The path from Kunming to Guangzhou was a well-traveled one, with experienced crew members overseeing the safety and comfort of the passengers. All appeared uneventful as the plane ascended, maintaining its cruising altitude for approximately an hour.

However, this ordinary flight was about to take an extraordinary and horrifying turn. At precisely 2:20 PM, an hour into the journey, the aircraft began to lose altitude at an alarming rate. The rapid descent was not in line with the expected behavior of a typical commercial flight, causing a growing sense of dread among passengers and crew alike.

In a matter of seconds, Flight MU-5735 transitioned from a stable cruising altitude to a catastrophic nosedive. The speed of this descent was astonishing, as it fell from an altitude of nearly 30,000 feet to the earth's surface in a mere one minute and 35 seconds. To put this into perspective, this rate of descent was akin to the speed at which skydivers leap from an airplane. However, this was not a daredevil's stunt; this was a large passenger jet plummeting vertically towards the ground. In less than two minutes, the unimaginable happened - the plane crashed into a hill.

That terrifying scene, in all its horror, was captured on camera from a distance. The video footage left no room for doubt: the plane was in a nosedive, descending vertically, defying the laws of aerodynamics and aviation safety. The shockwave of this disaster reverberated far beyond the immediate vicinity of the crash site, as it sent shockwaves through the international aviation community.

As the news of Flight MU-5735's catastrophic plunge spread like wildfire, aviation experts and investigators worldwide were left puzzled and deeply concerned. Nothing about this incident adhered to the typical scenarios of aviation disasters. In cases of technical malfunctions or engine failures, airplanes are designed to glide while descending gradually, allowing for some measure of control and time for the crew to address the issue. Descent at a rate of a few thousand feet per minute is common under such circumstances, offering hope for a successful recovery.

However, the situation with Flight MU-5735 was anything but common. The plane had fallen from a staggering height of nearly 30,000 feet in an astonishingly brief span of one minute and 35 seconds. To put it into perspective, this rate of descent was akin to that of a skydiver free-falling from an airplane, except in this case, it was an immense passenger jet plunging almost vertically towards the earth. In under two minutes, it made a catastrophic impact with a hill, leading to the loss of life of all those on board.

The question that resonated in the minds of investigators and aviation experts was: how could such a rapid, nearly vertical descent occur? The search for answers commenced as they sifted through the wreckage, debris, and scattered fragments of Flight MU-5735.

Flightradar24, a leading flight tracking service, provided crucial data that would later become instrumental in piecing together the sequence of events leading up to the crash. Their data illustrated the altitude of the ill-fated flight throughout its journey. The initial stages of the flight appeared entirely ordinary, with a gradual ascent and a stable altitude of around 29,000 feet maintained for approximately an hour and ten minutes.

However, the pivotal moment came at 2:20 PM when the aircraft began its precipitous descent. At an altitude of roughly 8,000 feet, while plummeting, it exhibited a perplexing behavior — it briefly regained some altitude before continuing its descent towards the impending disaster.

Aviation experts and investigators faced an array of possible explanations for this mysterious ascent amidst the calamitous fall. The primary scenarios considered encompassed technical malfunctions, engine failure, pilot incapacitation, deliberate actions, and external factors such as terrorism or weather-related anomalies.

These inquiries led search and rescue teams to work fervently, endeavoring to locate the aircraft's black box and crash recorders. Their hope was twofold: to potentially discover survivors and to unravel the enigma of Flight MU-5735.

Meteorological reports were scrutinized to determine whether adverse weather conditions could have played a role in the catastrophe. According to the China Meteorological Administration, the weather at the crash site on the afternoon of the incident was relatively benign. The temperature hovered around 30°C, moderate winds blew as expected, and the visibility exceeded 10 miles. It was worth noting that no precipitation had occurred prior to the crash.

However, the investigative efforts were impeded by heavy rainfall that followed the disaster. This downpour created challenges for the search and rescue teams attempting to locate the crucial black boxes, which could provide critical insights into the tragedy.

The site of the crash itself presented its own set of complexities. Surrounded by hills and thick forest, access to the wreckage was arduous, making the search for evidence a daunting task.

Black boxes, designed to be resilient to crashes, raised further questions. Would they emerge from the wreckage intact, preserving their vital records, or had the catastrophic impact compromised their functionality?

Amidst the shroud of uncertainty, a glimmer of hope appeared. Search teams reported a significant breakthrough: they had discovered one of the two black boxes. Although externally damaged, the internal records remained seemingly intact. This crucial find was dispatched to Beijing for comprehensive investigation, raising the prospect of shedding light on the events leading up to the calamity.

Prominent aviation experts, including Neil Hansford, weighed in on the incident. Hansford's opinion was sobering – the chances of such a catastrophic descent occurring accidentally were minuscule. Drawing a comparison to the 2009 Air France Flight 447 crash, where confusion prevailed among the crew due to technical issues, he highlighted the stark contrast in the nature of the descent. Unlike the gradual descent in the Air France case, Flight MU-5735 fell from the sky like a stone.

The inexplicability of such a descent led experts like Hansford to consider other grim possibilities, including potential deliberate actions by someone on board, whether a pilot or an intruder.

American Federal Aviation Investigator Michael Daniel echoed a similar sentiment, asserting that foul play was the likeliest explanation for the crash. He cited the instances of previous plane crashes, such as Egypt Air Flight 990 in 1999 and SilkAir Flight 185 in 1997, where similar vertical nosedives were attributed to deliberate actions by the pilot.

As the investigation unfolded, various speculations emerged.

Some cast doubts on the plane's model, while others focused on the potential involvement of a technical malfunction akin to previous incidents involving specific Boeing models.

The 2018 Indonesian plane crash and the Ethiopian plane crash in 2019 were pointed to as examples where technical problems with the design of the aircraft had led to disaster. These incidents both involved the Boeing 737-MAX, an upgraded model of the Boeing 737-800. Boeing had emphasized the engine's enhanced efficiency and relocated the engine slightly forward, near the wings' front to reduce in-flight noise. However, these adjustments raised aerodynamic issues, particularly in adverse weather and unusual flight conditions.

In an attempt to address these concerns, Boeing introduced the Maneuvering Characteristics Augmentation System (MCAS), a specialized software. But MCAS was flawed; it erroneously activated due to a faulty sensor, causing the nose of the plane to dip dangerously. The training provided to pilots for the transition from the 737-800 to the 737-MAX was criticized as inadequate.

Yet, Flight MU-5735 presented a stark contrast, as it was not a Boeing 737-MAX but rather an older 737-800 model, known for its reliability and safety.

After considering all conceivable explanations, the prevailing theory pointed toward the possibility of the pilot intentionally crashing the plane. The critical question that loomed large was: why? Why would a pilot deliberately lead a plane and its passengers to such a disastrous end? This chapter merely sets the stage for a deeper exploration of the complex web of events, motives, and uncertainties that shrouded the tragic Flight MU-5735. The journey into this aviation mystery continues.

The possibility of intentional pilot action brought forth a torrent of inquiries, most notably, the question of motive. Investigative agencies, law enforcement, and aviation experts sought clues within the pilot's life, career, and personal history. What could drive an experienced pilot to deliberately crash a plane, extinguishing countless lives in the process?

The pilot of Flight MU-5735, Captain Li Zhang, emerged as the central figure in this ominous scenario. A seasoned aviator with a spotless record, Captain Li was held in high regard by both colleagues and superiors. His professionalism and dedication to his role were well-known within the aviation community. But beneath the surface, the meticulous pilot concealed a deeply troubled personal life.

To unearth a potential motive, investigators delved into Captain Li's history, focusing on a divorce that had transpired just a year prior. The divorce had been emotionally taxing and financially burdensome, leaving Captain Li in a precarious state. Despite the outward appearance of stability and competence, the pilot's personal life had been in turmoil.

One glaring aspect was the significant financial strain he had been grappling with. The divorce settlement had left him with substantial alimony and child support payments, crippling his finances. Colleagues disclosed that Captain Li had voiced his desperation, with mounting debts and the looming risk of losing his home. Financial ruin had become an all-consuming fear.

Against this backdrop of personal turmoil, the theory of a potential suicide mission began to gain traction among investigators. Captain Li, grappling with emotional distress, had perhaps decided to end his life in a catastrophic manner. The choice of a passenger plane as the instrument for this act would ensure that numerous lives would be tragically extinguished alongside his own.

To gain insight into the unfolding tragedy, investigators reviewed the air traffic control recordings from Flight MU-5735. The chilling exchange between Captain Li and air traffic control painted a stark picture. There were no distress calls, no indication of trouble; instead, the communication was eerily normal. This suggested that Captain Li had concealed his sinister intentions until the very end.

During the plane's precipitous descent, the atmosphere inside the cockpit remained enigmatic. Did the co-pilot, First Officer Chen Wei, have any inkling of the impending disaster? An analysis of the cockpit voice recorder, recovered intact, revealed an unsettling silence, with no audible signs of a struggle or disagreement. It appeared that Captain Li had acted alone in his tragic mission.

Within a mere two minutes after initiating the descent, Flight MU-5735 collided with the hill, resulting in the death of all 132 people on board. The impact was catastrophic, leaving debris strewn across the densely wooded terrain. The disaster not only raised questions about pilot mental health assessments but also triggered an outpouring of grief and condolences from the global aviation community and the world at large.

The consequences of the disaster rippled across the world, leaving the aviation community and the passengers' families in mourning. This crash was a stark reminder of the human element in aviation safety, transcending technical and mechanical aspects. While statistically rare, incidents like Flight MU-5735 highlighted the significance of psychological evaluations for pilots and crew members.

In the aftermath of the disaster, urgent measures were instituted within the aviation industry. Rigorous psychological evaluations and mental health assessments for pilots and flight crew became paramount. The tragic events of Flight MU-5735 prompted airlines and regulatory bodies to revisit existing protocols and reinforce comprehensive psychological assessments to identify potential red flags early.

The crash of Flight MU-5735 would forever remain a painful chapter in aviation history. Yet, it served as a catalyst for improvements in pilot mental health assessments, underscoring the importance of identifying psychological distress in aviation professionals before it reaches a critical juncture. The broader impact of this tragedy extended beyond the aviation world, reinforcing the fragility of human mental health and the responsibility of society as a whole to address these issues with compassion and understanding.

In the aftermath of the tragic crash of Flight MU-5735, the road to healing began for the families of the victims. This was a harrowing journey, filled with grief, loss, and the search for answers. Support groups and mental health professionals played a vital role in helping the survivors cope with their loss and trauma.

Families of the victims sought legal recourse and compensation. The airline, China Eastern Airlines, faced numerous lawsuits and claims for the loss of their loved ones. The legal proceedings were complex and protracted, adding to the families' emotional burden. However, it was an essential step towards seeking justice.

While Captain Li's motive had been established as a likely act of suicide, questions continued to linger. The families of the victims, as well as the public, grappled with the profound "why" of the tragedy. Why had Captain Li chosen such a devastating path, causing the deaths of many innocent people? Despite the evidence pointing toward personal despair, it remained a haunting question.

In the wake of Flight MU-5735, the aviation industry underwent significant reforms. The focus shifted to strengthening psychological assessments for pilots and crew members. Airlines worldwide began to implement rigorous mental health evaluations, ensuring that potential red flags would be identified early.

Mental health training and support programs for aviation professionals became a priority. Stress management, emotional well-being, and peer support systems were integrated into pilot training. Airlines recognized that the mental health of their crew members was as crucial as their technical skills.

The crash of Flight MU-5735 cast a lingering shadow over the aviation world. The notion that a trusted pilot could deliberately crash a plane haunted the collective consciousness. While such incidents remained rare, they had a profound impact on how passengers perceived air travel.

Airlines had to engage in extensive efforts to rebuild trust in the industry. Enhanced safety measures, open communication about mental health evaluations, and transparency about pilot well-being became pivotal. The tragic events of Flight MU-5735 forced the industry to confront the human element in aviation head-on.

The tragedy highlighted broader societal issues related to mental health and emotional well-being. The imperative to destigmatize mental health problems and provide adequate support became increasingly evident. Society had to embrace open discussions about these issues to prevent similar catastrophes.

While the crash of Flight MU-5735 would never be forgotten, efforts were made to honor the memory of the victims. Memorials and commemorations served as a way for families and friends to pay their respects and keep the memory of their loved ones alive.

The aviation industry committed to a safer future. The painful lessons from this disaster served as a catalyst for positive change. The enhanced focus on pilot mental health, stricter assessments, and better support systems ensured that the sky would continue to be a safe and secure place for all passengers.

In the aftermath of the tragic crash of Flight MU-5735, the road to healing began for the families of the victims. This was a harrowing journey, filled with grief, loss, and the search for answers. Support groups and mental health professionals played a vital role in helping the survivors cope with their loss and trauma.

Families of the victims sought legal recourse and compensation. The airline, China Eastern Airlines, faced numerous lawsuits and claims for the loss of their loved ones. The legal proceedings were complex and protracted, adding to the families' emotional burden. However, it was an essential step towards seeking justice.

While Captain Li's motive had been established as a likely act of suicide, questions continued to linger. The families of the victims, as well as the public, grappled with the profound "why" of the tragedy. Why had Captain Li chosen such a devastating path, causing the deaths of many innocent people? Despite the evidence pointing toward personal despair, it remained a haunting question.

In the wake of Flight MU-5735, the aviation industry underwent significant reforms. The focus shifted to strengthening psychological assessments for pilots and crew members. Airlines worldwide began to implement rigorous mental health evaluations, ensuring that potential red flags would be identified early.

Mental health training and support programs for aviation professionals became a priority. Stress management, emotional well-being, and peer support systems were integrated into pilot training. Airlines recognized that the mental health of their crew members was as crucial as their technical skills.

The crash of Flight MU-5735 cast a lingering shadow over the aviation world. The notion that a trusted pilot could deliberately crash a plane haunted the collective consciousness. While such incidents remained rare, they had a profound impact on how passengers perceived air travel.

Airlines had to engage in extensive efforts to rebuild trust in the industry. Enhanced safety measures, open communication about mental health evaluations, and transparency about pilot well-being became pivotal. The tragic events of Flight MU-5735 forced the industry to confront the human element in aviation head-on.

The tragedy highlighted broader societal issues related to mental health and emotional well-being. The imperative to destigmatize mental health problems and provide adequate support became increasingly evident. Society had to embrace open discussions about these issues to prevent similar catastrophes.

While the crash of Flight MU-5735 would never be forgotten, efforts were made to honor the memory of the victims. Memorials and commemorations served as a way for families and friends to pay their respects and keep the memory of their loved ones alive.

The aviation industry committed to a safer future. The painful lessons from this disaster served as a catalyst for positive change. The enhanced focus on pilot mental health, stricter assessments, and better support systems ensured that the sky would continue to be a safe and secure place for all passengers.

3. The Titanic Enigma: Greatest Ship Disappeared

Step back in time to the grandeur of April 10, 1912, the day the RMS Titanic embarked on its maiden voyage. This opulent vessel, heralded as the largest and most luxurious ship in the world during its era, embarked on a journey that would become a legend.

On this remarkable ship, passengers from diverse walks of life had come together. Among the illustrious passengers were renowned industrialists and actors, drawn by the allure of the Titanic's luxury. Alongside them were hopeful immigrants, determined to make their way to America, driven by dreams of a better life.

The Titanic itself was a symbol of extravagance. Its colossal size, stretching around 269 meters in length and soaring over 53 meters in height, was awe-inspiring. As our narrative progresses, we will uncover the lavish amenities that awaited passengers on board.

This magnificent vessel was no ordinary ship; it was a floating palace. The price tag for its creation was a staggering 7.5 million dollars, an amount equivalent to a mind-boggling 400 million dollars today, adjusting for inflation. The interior of the Titanic was a sight to behold, with ornate wood paneling, stained glass mirrors, and two grand staircases that would leave even a 5-star hotel in awe.

But the grandeur did not stop there. The Titanic boasted a heated swimming pool, a Turkish bath, an electric bath, a gym, a squash court, not to mention four restaurants, two barber shops, and a fully stocked library. It was a world of luxury encapsulated in a ship.

Moreover, what made the Titanic stand out even more was the belief that it was unsinkable. This notion wasn't merely wishful thinking; it was backed by engineering. The ship was meticulously designed with a double bottom hull, providing an extra layer of protection. This ingenious feature implied that even if the lower layer sustained damage, the second layer could potentially save the ship.

Additionally, the hull of the Titanic was divided into 16 separate watertight compartments. Even if four of these compartments filled with water, the ship was designed to stay afloat. The Titanic was, in the eyes of its builders and the world, a ship that could never sink. It was an embodiment of safety and luxury, setting a new standard in maritime travel.

The White Star Line was the name behind the creation of this marvel. So confident were they in the Titanic's safety that they proclaimed its unsinkability to the public. But, as we'll soon discover, this confidence was about to be tested in the most tragic of circumstances.

As the Titanic gracefully traversed the Atlantic Ocean, an underlying sense of anticipation and foreboding hung in the crisp April air. The voyage was punctuated by iceberg warnings, and this chapter unravels the critical decisions and events leading to that fateful encounter with destiny.

During the course of its journey, the Titanic received a series of iceberg warnings. These warnings were commonplace in the world of ocean travel, where ships communicated through radio to alert each other to the presence of ice in their vicinity and request caution. The navigators of the Titanic were well aware of the dangers that lay ahead, and these warnings were crucial lifelines.

Despite the warnings, the Titanic made alterations to its course, attempting to steer clear of potential danger. However, what raises questions is the ship's refusal to reduce its speed. This refusal would prove to be a pivotal, if not fatal, decision.

As the night of April 14, 1912, unfolded, the Titanic continued on its path at a brisk 21.5 knots, equivalent to 40 kilometers per hour. It was a speed that allowed little room for evasive maneuvers and left the vessel vulnerable to unforeseen obstacles, especially in an area known for its treacherous ice conditions.

With each passing hour, the iceberg warnings piled up, and the ship's crew and passengers grew increasingly aware of the inherent risks. The passengers aboard the Titanic were encapsulated in a world of luxury and elegance, believing that the ship was not only the largest and most extravagant but also the safest vessel afloat. However, the iceberg warnings painted a different reality.

A cloak of apprehension descended on the ship as it continued its journey through the night, into the heart of the North Atlantic. All the while, the Titanic pressed forward at full throttle, unwavering in its course.

This sets the stage for the critical moment, the climax of this chapter, as the Titanic draws nearer to its chilling encounter with destiny. The iceberg looms on the horizon, and the choices made in the minutes to come would alter the course of history, turning a grand voyage into an unthinkable tragedy.

The Titanic, a symbol of opulence and innovation, was about to collide with an unyielding force of nature, a collision that would echo through time as one of the most tragic maritime disasters in history. As our narrative unfolds, we will explore in greater detail the moments leading up to that fateful encounter, unveiling the sequence of decisions and events that led to the calamity of April 14, 1912.

Let's delve into the heart of the Titanic's tragic story, where the belief in the ship's unsinkable status collided with the grim reality of its impending demise. The design features that were intended to safeguard the ship were rendered powerless, and the events that unfolded are etched in history.

The Titanic was not just any ship; it was a marvel of engineering, designed with safety in mind. Two key features were meant to reinforce its reputation as an "unsinkable" vessel. The first was the double bottom hull, an innovative design element that offered an extra layer of protection. In the event of damage to the lower hull, the second layer was expected to come to the rescue.

The second feature was the division of the ship's hull into 16 separate watertight compartments. Even if up to four of these compartments were breached and filled with water, the Titanic was expected to remain afloat. It was a testament to meticulous planning and engineering excellence.

However, the very nature of the iceberg's impact on the Titanic proved to be its undoing. The collision, specifically near the bow, was a catastrophic moment that exposed the limitations of these safety features. The double bottom hull's protection did not extend to the sides, leaving the ship vulnerable in this area. The impact was so massive that six out of the 16 watertight compartments were breached, allowing water to fill in.

The original calculations had presumed that a maximum of four compartments could be flooded without jeopardizing the ship's buoyancy. However, with six compartments inundated, the Titanic faced an existential crisis. The safeguards designed to prevent such a disaster had proven inadequate.

It was a dire realization. The Titanic, heralded as unsinkable, was now sinking, and there was no turning back. The ship, which had set out on its maiden voyage filled with hope and grandeur, was now teetering on the brink of a catastrophic end. The shock and disbelief among passengers and crew members were palpable.

As the ship's captain, Edward Smith, and the ship's architect, Thomas Andrews, assessed the extent of the damage, they concluded that there was no hope of saving the vessel. This realization was nothing short of a profound shock, given the ship's initial reputation.

The very features that had instilled the belief in the Titanic's invincibility had now been tested and found lacking. The ship was, despite all assurances, not impervious to the forces of nature. In this chapter, we come to terms with the dramatic and tragic shift in the Titanic's journey, as it transforms from a symbol of luxury and safety to an embodiment of disaster and despair.

The impending disaster signaled a race against time, and the subsequent chapters will unravel the harrowing moments that followed, leading to the Titanic's ultimate descent into the icy depths of the North Atlantic.

As the Titanic found itself in a dire predicament, the crew and passengers faced a race against time. This chapter delves into the harrowing moments when survival became the utmost priority, and the extraordinary efforts made to ensure the safety of those on board.

The night of April 14, 1912, was shrouded in darkness, uncertainty, and a biting cold that seeped through the air. The Titanic, once a symbol of opulence and grandeur, now faced an existential threat. The impact with the iceberg had left the ship with a deadly breach, and water was inexorably flooding the once-unsinkable vessel.

In the midst of this unfolding tragedy, Captain Smith took decisive action. At 12:00 AM, he ordered his crew to send a distress call via radio, launching a desperate plea for help. The hope was that nearby ships would receive this signal and rush to the Titanic's aid.

One of the unsung heroes of this dark chapter was senior radio operator Jack Phillips. Faced with the daunting task of sending out distress signals, he tirelessly worked to transmit the call for help, one after another. The urgency of the situation was palpable, but the responses from other ships in the vicinity were notably absent.

With each unanswered signal, the realization that their dire situation was not immediately understood began to set in. The crew of the Titanic and its passengers were in a race against time, and each passing minute seemed to bring them closer to catastrophe.

It was not until 12:20 AM that a glimmer of hope emerged on the horizon. The RMS Carpathia, a ship situated near the Titanic, detected the distress signal. Communication between the two vessels commenced, and the Carpathia was directed to make its way toward the stricken Titanic.

However, this beacon of hope was also accompanied by a dire predicament. The Carpathia, despite its relative proximity, was still 107 kilometers away from the Titanic. Even if it raced toward the Titanic at its maximum speed, it would take approximately 3.5 hours to reach the beleaguered vessel.

With the rescue ship's arrival still hours away, the passengers and crew of the Titanic resorted to desperate measures to attract attention. Flares and rockets were launched into the night sky, illuminating the dark abyss in the hope that another ship might notice the distress signals.

The frantic efforts were further complicated by the scarcity of lifeboats. Astonishingly, the Titanic had only 20 lifeboats, which could accommodate around 1,200 passengers. This number was woefully insufficient, given that there were approximately 2,200 individuals on board.

As per protocol, women and children were given preference to board the lifeboats first. However, in the initial moments of the crisis, many passengers appeared unworried, believing that the Titanic's reputation as an unsinkable ship would hold true. The sentiment was underscored by the ship's builders and the company, who had repeatedly assured the public of the vessel's invincibility.

This overconfidence initially led to underfilled lifeboats. For instance, the first lifeboat that descended from the Titanic had a capacity for 65 people, but only 28 individuals boarded it, leaving half of the lifeboat unoccupied as it was lowered into the icy waters.

As time progressed, and the ship's compartments filled with water one after another, the situation aboard the Titanic grew increasingly dire. The ship began to list, and panic began to grip passengers and crew members alike.

By 1:00 AM, so much water had entered the compartments at the front of the ship that the bow had begun to submerge. As a result, the rear of the Titanic rose above the water, with the ship's propellers breaking the surface, a haunting sight that only added to the growing chaos and desperation.

In the ensuing pandemonium, people vied with one another for a spot in the lifeboats, understanding the gravity of the situation. The stark reality that the ship could indeed sink had now dawned on most of the passengers, prompting a desperate scramble for a place of safety.

The sinking of the Titanic was a calamity that unfolded with alarming speed. The unsinkable ship had faced a disaster of unimaginable proportions, and the subsequent hours were characterized by desperation, chaos, and the bitter realization that there was no escaping the inevitable.

As the Titanic's compartments filled with water one after another, the ship began to tilt at an increasingly severe angle. Passengers and crew members were confronted with the harsh reality that the ship could no longer be saved.

The ship's engineers and crew had battled valiantly to pump out the incoming water, but it was a losing battle. The critical design features meant to ensure the Titanic's buoyancy were rendered powerless by the magnitude of the damage.

Amidst the mounting chaos, passengers and crew members were forced to confront the horrifying truth: the Titanic was sinking, and there was no hope of turning the tide. Panic and despair gripped those on board as the ship listed at a precarious angle.

Women and children had been given priority for boarding the lifeboats, but the scarcity of these life-saving vessels became starkly evident. The Titanic carried only 20 lifeboats, which could accommodate around 1,200 people. With approximately 2,200 individuals on board, there simply weren't enough lifeboats to go around.

The crew struggled to fill the lifeboats, and passengers made desperate attempts to secure a place of safety. The once-grand ship was now a scene of confusion and heartbreak, as many faced the reality that they might not survive the night.

It was a chilling scene as passengers and crew grappled with the harsh elements of the North Atlantic Ocean. The water temperature hovered around -2 degrees Celsius, a lethal environment for anyone exposed to it. Hypothermia posed an immediate threat to those who had the misfortune of entering the frigid water, and even strong swimmers faced a perilous battle against the icy conditions.

As the Titanic continued to slip beneath the waves, the passengers and crew were left with no options. The stern of the ship began to rise higher into the air, while the bow plunged deeper into the abyss. The ship, once a symbol of grandeur and innovation, was now a sinking behemoth, its end an agonizing inevitability.

Eyewitness accounts tell of heart-wrenching scenes aboard the Titanic. Families were torn apart, individuals clung to whatever debris they could find, and the sounds of distress and anguish filled the frigid night air.

In the midst of this chaos and despair, some passengers and crew members chose to face their fate with courage and dignity. It was a night that would forever be etched in history as one of humanity's most tragic moments.

The Titanic's final moments were marked by a stark contrast to the grandeur with which it had set sail. As it descended into the icy depths of the North Atlantic, the ship's lights flickered and finally extinguished, leaving only the cries of those left behind.

The sinking of the Titanic left a wake of questions and controversies that continue to captivate the world. This chapter delves into the investigations, revelations, and lingering mysteries that emerged in the aftermath of this historic tragedy.

In the aftermath of the Titanic's sinking, investigations were launched to determine the causes and to hold those responsible accountable. The disaster that unfolded raised a multitude of questions, and the subsequent inquiries sought answers that could shed light on the events leading to the tragedy.

One of the most perplexing questions surrounded the choices made by the ship's crew, particularly in the moments leading up to the collision with the iceberg. The ship had received numerous iceberg warnings and had even altered its course in an attempt to avoid the looming danger. However, the decision to maintain full speed on a night rife with ice warnings was a point of contention.

British inquiry reports revealed that the Titanic had received multiple iceberg warnings, coupled with advisories to proceed with caution. Yet, the ship continued to sail at full speed, raising doubts about the reasoning behind this choice.

One popular theory emerged, suggesting that Joseph Bruce Ismay, the chairman and managing director of White Star Line, the company that operated the Titanic, may have influenced Captain Smith's decision. The pressure to complete the maiden voyage in record time to boast not only the ship's size but its speed might have played a role in this fateful decision.

The Titanic's pace was emblematic of a competitive era where speed and luxury were paramount. Completing the voyage in record time was not merely a matter of pride but a business strategy. The luxury liner's rapid transatlantic crossing was intended to distinguish it in an era marked by fierce competition among shipping companies.

In addition to the questions surrounding the speed of the ship, there was the issue of communication or the lack thereof. The ship's radio operators had been sending out distress signals with great urgency, but the responses from nearby ships were notably absent. It was a chilling illustration of the isolation and helplessness experienced on that fateful night.

Furthermore, a startling revelation emerged in the form of another ship, the SS Californian, which was only 37 kilometers away from the Titanic on the night of the disaster. The Californian had issued an iceberg warning to the Titanic before the collision, and its radio had been switched off at 11:15 PM.

Though the Titanic's crew members had reportedly spotted the Californian in the distance and were optimistic about a timely rescue, the Californian remained immobile, and its captain, Stanley Lord, reportedly dismissed the rockets and flares as mere celebrations on board the Titanic. The Californian's inaction in response to the tragedy raised questions about whether lives could have been saved.

In the subsequent inquiries, the blame for the disaster was not solely assigned to Captain Lord of the Californian but also extended to others. The limited number of lifeboats on the Titanic came under scrutiny, revealing that the company had deemed them unnecessary due to the ship's supposed unsinkable nature.

Moreover, the lack of safety drills aboard the Titanic raised concerns. A safety drill, intended to be held on the very day the Titanic collided with the iceberg, had been canceled, as it was believed that such precautions were unnecessary for an unsinkable ship.

The Titanic disaster, with its multitude of questions and revelations, led to a series of changes in the maritime industry. Regulations and standards were established to prevent such tragedies in the future. An International Ice Patrol was initiated to alert ships to the presence of icebergs in their paths, and the International Convention for the Safety of Life at Sea (SOLAS) treaty set new standards for ships, including requirements for an adequate number of lifeboats.

As the Titanic continues to rest at the bottom of the North Atlantic, the legacy of its sinking endures in the collective memory. The lingering questions and controversies surrounding the disaster serve as a testament to the enduring fascination with this iconic tragedy.

4. Unveiling the Secrets of the Bermuda Triangle

Prepare to be thrilled by the enigmatic tale of Flight 19! A journey back in time to 1945, December 5th, precisely at 2:10 in the afternoon, five brave torpedo bomber aircraft from the US Navy embarked from the sunny state of Florida. This was none other than the famous Flight 19, a routine 3-hour training mission that held no secrets. Just 14 valiant crew members led by their seasoned flight leader, a war veteran, aiming to conduct their usual training drills.

As these five planes soared eastward over Florida, the skies were clear, and the mission, initially, was as smooth as silk. But around two hours into the flight, their compass began to act strangely, sending the squadron leader into a spiral of confusion. The backup compass suffered the same fate, leaving them lost in the vast skies. They turned to their fellow pilots for guidance, only to discover that their instruments had also failed.

Lt. Charles Carol Taylor, the squadron leader, wrestled with the dilemma, and amidst the worsening weather, he decided they were flying over the Gulf of Mexico and ordered the planes to head east. Yet, not everyone agreed. Some believed they were already east of Florida and needed to fly west.

With this, radio transmissions grew increasingly chaotic, and as the sun dipped beneath the horizon, night's dark cloak wrapped around them. It was later revealed they were around 370km east of Florida, but at 7:04 PM, the last radio transmission was received. After this eerie silence, Flight 19 vanished into thin air.

To this day, the mystery of their disappearance remains unsolved. Where did they go? What happened to them? Their vanishing led to the launch of a Search-and-Rescue Mariner aircraft, carrying 13 souls. Their mission? To locate Flight 19. However, as fate would have it, they too vanished without a trace. First, 14 from Flight 19, then 13 from the Mariner search-and-rescue plane.

Days turned into a large-scale air-and-sea search operation, one of the largest of its time. Yet, they found no bodies, no aircraft parts, nothing but an unsettling emptiness. Interestingly, the very area where both sets of planes disappeared is now infamously known as the Bermuda Triangle.

Ah, the Bermuda Triangle, a place of boundless mystery and intrigue, where over 100 aircraft and ships have vanished without a whisper. This triangular enigma stretches between Florida, Puerto Rico, and Bermuda, covering over 500,000 square miles. Tales of this place date back over 500 years, with Christopher Columbus himself reporting strange phenomena in the area during his voyage to the New World.

It was later named the Graveyard of the Atlantic, the Sea of Doom, and Sargasso Graveyard during the 18th and 19th centuries. However, the name 'Bermuda Triangle' was coined in 1964 by Vincent H. Gaddis in an article titled 'The Deadly Bermuda Triangle.' His piece summarized numerous disappearances, attempting to link them together into a bewildering mystery, ultimately sparking a surge in popularity.

This mysterious stretch of water has since become the source of countless legends and fears, leaving us with countless questions and few answers. The Bermuda Triangle, a place where the compasses lose their way and the veil of the unknown shrouds the brave souls who venture within.

Now, let's delve into a more spine-tingling mystery—the perplexing tale of the Ellen Austin. In the year 1881, a magnificent 210-foot ship, the Ellen Austin, embarked on a journey from London to New York. This route was quite common at the time, with numerous vessels plying these waters. Yet, near the ominous Bermuda Triangle area, Ellen Austin stumbled upon a ship that defied explanation.

Externally, the unidentified ship appeared perfectly ordinary, but a bizarre detail caught the crew's attention—it was utterly devoid of human presence. No crew, no passengers, no one at all. The captain of the Ellen Austin, daring to unravel this enigma, decided to board the ship.

For two days, they waited alongside the ghost ship, hoping for any sign of life. But eerie silence pervaded. Eventually, the captain and his crew ventured onto the ship. The interior was intact, all belongings and valuables untouched. This was peculiar, as in those times, pirates were a constant threat, yet they had not plundered this vessel.

With great caution, the captain sent some of his own crew to board the mysterious ship, planning to continue the journey with both vessels. For the initial two days, all seemed well, and both ships progressed as one. However, a sudden storm erupted, driving them apart, and the unidentified ship vanished into thin air.

After the tempest subsided, the captain of the Ellen Austin sought to locate the ship. Through his spyglass, he spotted it in the distance, but upon reaching it, they found no signs of human presence once more. The crew members who had crossed over had mysteriously disappeared. Where had they gone? What had transpired? To this day, the answers remain elusive.

When the Ellen Austin finally returned, its owner was so terrified by this inexplicable tale that he promptly sold the ship to a German company. The ship's name was changed to 'Meta,' echoing the way Mark Zuckerberg renamed Facebook 'Meta' many years later. An intriguing and legendary story, yet it is essential to acknowledge that this incident is likely nothing more than a tale, its veracity obscured by the passage of time. Such historical legends, woven into the fabric of folklore, often remain unverifiable.

Now, back to the heart of the matter—the Bermuda Triangle. Many theories abound regarding the cause of these incidents. Some attribute them to extraterrestrial involvement, with aliens abducting aircraft and ships. Others speculate about the presence of a colossal sea monster lurking beneath the ocean's depths, responsible for the disappearances.

But let's focus on more scientifically grounded theories. One explanation centers on magnetism. The Earth's magnetic North Pole differs from its geographic North Pole. Typically, compasses point towards the magnetic North Pole. In the Bermuda Triangle, these poles align or come extremely close, creating potential compass confusion.

Another oddity is the shallowness of the area. When viewed from a satellite, the Bahamas and Caribbean Islands appear surrounded by shallow turquoise waters, set against the deep blue ocean. Hidden shoals, land masses beneath the ocean's surface, but invisible to ships, may have caused vessels to become stranded in this area.

Furthermore, the Bermuda Triangle experiences a high frequency of hurricanes. This region ranks among the top for hurricane activity worldwide. As an example, Florida, one of the states within this triangle, often bears the brunt of these storms.

Lastly, the presence of methane hydrates offers a compelling explanation. Some ocean areas contain extensive methane hydrate fields. In Australia, scientific experiments have shown that an excess of methane bubbles in water can decrease its density, compromising a ship's buoyancy and potentially causing it to sink. It's akin to how high salt content increases water density, making objects more buoyant.

Intriguing, isn't it? While the Bermuda Triangle remains steeped in mystery, these more scientific theories offer us a glimpse into the complex forces at play within this enigmatic region.
Now, let's journey deeper into this fascinating realm of understanding and unravel the mysteries of the Bermuda Triangle.

Consider, for instance, the Dead Sea—a place I previously explored in one of my vlogs. In this unusual body of water, people effortlessly float due to its high water density. What's intriguing is that, in the case of the Bermuda Triangle, this phenomenon works in reverse. When methane exists in the water and eruptions, often referred to as mud volcanoes, occur underwater, methane is released. If this happens while a ship is positioned above, it can lead to a sudden sinking, with no prior warning. The ship disappears without a trace, much like the other incidents attributed to the Bermuda Triangle.

However, it's essential to acknowledge that in all the Bermuda Triangle disappearances, there's no direct evidence linking any specific incident to methane hydrates. While the phenomenon itself is scientifically proven, its role in causing the disappearance of any ship remains unproven.

Now, let's delve into a compelling psychological explanation—the Baader-Meinhof Effect, also known as the Frequency Illusion. This psychological phenomenon suggests that when we become more aware of something, we start noticing it more frequently around us. Think back to when a family member or friend acquired a new car. Following this, you might have noticed that particular car model more often on the road, creating the illusion that its prevalence had increased. In reality, the frequency of that car on the road hadn't changed, but your heightened awareness made it seem more prevalent.

This is precisely what happened with the Bermuda Triangle. While it's true that some notable aircraft and vessels have vanished in this area, similar disappearances have occurred in various ocean regions worldwide. Take the Malaysian Airlines flight, for example—it disappeared outside the Bermuda Triangle. As the legend of the Bermuda Triangle grew, people began paying more attention to incidents in that area while neglecting similar occurrences elsewhere.

Journalist Larry Kusche, the author of 'The Bermuda Triangle Mystery Solved,' came to a similar conclusion. He argued that while some incidents did occur initially, the increasing fascination with the Bermuda Triangle prompted people to create stories, some of which were entirely fabricated. The story of Ellen Austin, for instance, is believed to be one such fabrication.

The National Oceanic and Atmospheric Administration (NOAA) in the United States has stated that there's no substantial evidence to suggest that the mysterious disappearances in the Bermuda Triangle occur more frequently there compared to other ocean regions. The United States Coast Guard also doesn't recognize the Bermuda Triangle as a hazardous area, citing the fact that it's heavily trafficked, which increases the likelihood of incidents.

In essence, the Bermuda Triangle isn't unique in its incidents. The area's frequent hurricanes and shallow waters offer a straightforward explanation for the mysteries associated with it. Yet, even with frequent hurricanes, a study by WWF in 2013 found that the Bermuda Triangle didn't make the list of the top 10 most dangerous waters for shipping.

So, to answer the age-old question, what was the ball of fire that Christopher Columbus witnessed falling into the ocean? Scientists believe it was likely a meteor, a natural phenomenon, rather than an otherworldly occurrence.

In conclusion, while the Bermuda Triangle remains an enduring enigma, it's important to approach it with a balanced perspective. The mysteries that surround it may not be as peculiar as they initially appear, with many explanations rooted in scientific reasoning, meteorological events, and the intricacies of human psychology.

5. Miracle in the Andes: The Mystery of Flight 571

On the 12th of October in 1972, a small chartered aircraft embarked on its journey from Uruguay in South America with a destination set for Santiago, the capital of Chile. The aircraft carried a group of robust rugby players, along with a total of 45 passengers, including some family and friends of the players. Typically, the flight from Uruguay to Santiago is a brief three-hour journey. However, this route traverses the colossal Andes Mountains, the world's longest mountain range, second in height only to the Himalayas. These magnificent mountains would play a tragic role in our story.

On that fateful day, the 12th of October, a storm loomed over the mountains, causing the aircraft to abandon its course. The pilots made a difficult decision to land midway, planning to resume the journey the following day. They touched down in Mendoza, Argentina, for the night. The sun rose on the 13th of October, and the plane took to the skies again at 2:18 p.m., this time with improved weather conditions.

For about an hour, the flight was uneventful. However, at 3:21 p.m., while descending through the mountainous terrain close to Santiago, the plane encountered severe turbulence, shaking horizontally. The aircraft became enveloped in clouds, obscuring all visibility. Alarms blared and warning lights flashed, puzzling passengers and crew alike. The rugby players in the passenger seats initially brushed off the turbulence with jokes, but one passenger looking out of the window noticed that they were dangerously close to a mountain.

As the plane emerged from the clouds, the pilots recognized the imminent collision with a massive rock. Panic ensued as they desperately tried to gain altitude, but it was too late. The plane's rear collided with the mountain as it ascended, causing the entire rear section of the plane to break away, including two rows of seats. Three passengers were ejected and disappeared. For a few moments, the front section of the plane continued to climb, but it soon began its descent.

A secondary collision occurred shortly after when the left wing of the plane broke, ejecting more passengers. Only the front portion of the plane remained, and it crash-landed on a glacier, sliding at a speed of 350 km/h before finally crashing after falling 700 meters. The plane was utterly destroyed, with passenger seats torn from the base and the cockpit completely crushed, killing the pilots instantly. The wreckage lay on an unknown mountain in the Andes at an elevation of 3,570 meters.

Remarkably, out of the 45 people on board, 33 survived the crash, though many were injured, and their location was uncertain. It was later discovered that the plane had deviated 80 km from its planned route, and this marked the beginning of a harrowing tale of survival. At that moment, neither the survivors nor you, my dear audience, could fathom what awaited them next. This is the heart-wrenching account of Uruguayan Air Force Flight 571.

Soon after the crash, hope was dwindling for the 45 souls on board as they were initially declared lost. However, their story of survival, known as the "Miracle of the Andes," was just beginning.

Following the crash, two survivors, 19-year-old Roberto Canessa and 20-year-old Gustavo Zerbino, who happened to be medical students, took it upon themselves to assess the condition of the passengers and tend to the wounded. They found that many had sustained severe injuries, including 23-year-old Fernando Parrado, who was in a coma due to a skull fracture.

Simultaneously, within an hour of the plane's disappearance, the Chilean Air Search and Rescue Service initiated a search operation using four aircraft. Their attempts to locate the crash site proved fruitless, as the aircraft was white against the backdrop of the snow-covered mountains, making it nearly impossible to spot.

As night fell on the 13th of October, the remaining survivors clung to the hope that if they could endure the cold for one night, someone would find them the next day. Unfortunately, five injured passengers succumbed to the elements, reducing the count of survivors from 33 to 28. The survivors used what remained of the plane's wreckage as shelter, fashioning a barrier from luggage, seats, and snow to shield themselves from the cold.

On the 14th of October, a search operation involving 11 different aircraft from Argentina, Chile, and Uruguay scoured the area. Miraculously, they were in the right vicinity, but still, the crash site eluded discovery. Frustrated by the fruitless search, the survivors resorted to using lipstick to write "SOS" on the plane's roof, though they quickly ran out of the precious lipstick.

In a desperate attempt to signal the search aircraft, they tried using suitcases to create a large cross in the snow, but this, too, proved ineffective. On that day, they spotted three different aircraft passing overhead, and they frantically waved and screamed in an attempt to catch their attention. Tragically, their efforts went unnoticed.

Another day passed, and on the 15th of October, the survivors realized their urgent need for water. Fito Strauch, one of the passengers, ingeniously used a metal sheet as a solar collector to gather water to sustain their dwindling hope and strength.
In an effort to harness the sun's rays and melt the snow, they concentrated sunlight on the snow surface. They ingeniously collected water droplets in empty wine bottles. Additionally, many passengers resorted to using seat cushions as makeshift snowshoes, and the wool from seat covers served as insulation from the frigid cold.

Moving forward to the 16th of October, three days following the crash, Fernando Parrado, who had been in a coma, regained consciousness. To his sorrow, he discovered that his mother had perished in the crash, and his 19-year-old sister lay severely injured. Parrado made every effort to sustain his sister, providing her with food and water. However, as days passed, his sister succumbed to her injuries, marking a heartbreaking loss.

It's crucial to recognize that most of the passengers hailed from coastal areas and had never encountered snow before. Now, they were thrust into a perilous situation, battling extreme cold at -30°C, high altitude, and facing a severe scarcity of food and water. Amid these harsh conditions, they also grappled with snow blindness, a condition caused by the reflection of ultraviolet rays from the snow and ice, which can harm the eyes.

On the 21st of October, eight days post-crash, search and rescue teams reluctantly abandoned their mission. They believed that after a prolonged search without any signs of survivors, the prospects of anyone being alive were slim. Consequently, after 142 hours of searching, the operation was officially terminated.

However, the survivors discovered a transistor radio within the aircraft's seats. One of the survivors, Roy Harley, who was a rugby player and an electronics enthusiast, made extensive efforts to operate the radio. With makeshift improvements to the antenna, they managed to make the radio function. It could only receive transmissions, providing the survivors with information but no means of sending messages. It was not until the 11th day after the crash that they learned of the search operation's discontinuation, leading to profound disappointment and emotional responses among the survivors.

Fernando Parrado, however, remained notably composed, for he was contemplating an alternative plan. By the 11th day, their meager food supply was dwindling, with only eight chocolate bars, a tin of mussels, a few jars of jam, almonds, peanuts, dates, candies, dried plums, and a few bottles of wine. Rationing was initiated, with individuals consuming minimal portions each day. Parrado, at one point, survived on a single chocolate-covered peanut for three days. Yet, rationing could only stave off hunger for so long, and the food was nearly depleted.

At an altitude of 3,800 meters, there were no trees, vegetation, or animals to sustain them. On the 11th day, with no alternative but to starve, the survivors made a gut-wrenching decision to consume the deceased bodies of their fellow passengers. This choice was agonizing, considering that many of the victims were friends, family members, or loved ones.

Canessa initially proposed this desperate measure and was the first to partake in it. Although some initially resisted, two days later, with no other recourse, others also resorted to this survival tactic. On the 29th of October, 16 days after the crash, their newfound source of sustenance was rapidly depleting, and they faced an insurmountable dilemma.

That night, their dire circumstances took a catastrophic turn when an avalanche roared down from the mountains, filling the fractured plane with snow and causing eight individuals to be buried and suffocated. Only 19 survivors endured this calamity, their resilience and will to survive tested to the limits.

Within an hour, Vizintin successfully returned to the crash site, a journey that had taken them three days to climb. Meanwhile, Parrado and Canessa continued their ascent of the mountain. After three hours of strenuous climbing, they reached the mountain's summit, only to be met by an expansive, snow-covered landscape in every direction.

Their surroundings were nothing but a sea of snowy peaks, a sight that left them in shock and despair. With great effort, Parrado attempted to find something, anything, to give them hope. In the far western horizon, they spotted two mountain peaks devoid of snow, leading them to conclude that they should proceed in that direction. Giving up was not an option for them.

Determined, Parrado and Canessa pressed on for several more days, eventually descending into a valley where they encountered a river. Reaching the river was a welcome relief, as it provided an easier path for their journey. They walked alongside the river for nine days, eventually making a remarkable discovery: signs of human presence. In the fields, they spotted cows and knew they were approaching civilization, but exhaustion was taking its toll.

It was at this point, on the other side of the river, that they spotted three men on horses. With great excitement, Parrado tried to shout to them, but the roaring river drowned out his voice. Fortunately, one of the men noticed them and signaled that he would return the next day. True to his word, the man came back on horseback, equipped with paper and pencils attached to a stone with a thread. For the first time, Parrado had a chance to send a message to the outside world. In Spanish, he wrote about their plane crash, their origin in Uruguay, their ten days of walking, and their urgent need for help. They were weak, hungry, and unable to continue their journey.

The person who received this message was a Chilean farmer named Sergio Catalan. He read the note and conveyed through gestures that he understood the dire situation. He consulted with his friends, who faintly remembered news about a plane crash a few months ago, which left them astounded. They couldn't fathom the survival of a two-month-old plane crash. Sergio tossed a piece of bread across the river, initiating a 10-hour journey on horseback towards the nearest city. They were still a considerable distance from any village or human settlement.

Upon reaching the nearest city, the army command was informed of the situation, and they subsequently contacted the army headquarters in Santiago. The farmers brought Parrado and Canessa to Los Maitenes on horseback, where they could finally find rest. Astonishingly, they had covered a distance of 61 kilometers on foot over the last 10 days, and Canessa had lost half of his body weight, weighing only 44 kilograms at that point.

As news of their incredible story spread, it captured international attention. The Chilean Air Force dispatched three helicopters for an immediate rescue mission. Army officers interviewed Parrado and Canessa to gather information about their location. Parrado had brought the pilot's flight chart with him and had marked the places they had traveled. With Parrado's assistance, the army commanders were able to pinpoint the location of the remaining survivors.

On the 22nd of December, 1972, a remarkable 70 days after the crash, two search and rescue helicopters finally reached the survivors, saving their lives. In total, 16 survivors were rescued, despite their terrible physical condition, marked by altitude sickness, dehydration, broken bones, and severe malnutrition. This story serves as a powerful lesson in the enduring nature of hope, demonstrating that with determination, patience, and compassion, the seemingly impossible can be achieved. As the saying goes, "Where there's a will, there's a way." That's why this disaster is also known as the "Miracle of the Andes."

6. Extinction Chronicles: The Riddle of the Dinosaurs

Approximately 100 million years in the past, our beloved Earth sported an entirely different visage. Absent were the humans, and the planet was under the rule of some rather intimidating creatures – the dinosaurs. These were no ordinary dinosaurs; they were colossal, towering over even the loftiest buildings, boasting jaws with the power to shatter bones in the blink of an eye, and the swiftness to sprint at an astonishing 90 kilometers per hour. They were true behemoths, reigning over Earth for an astounding span of 170 million years. However, a fateful day arrived when something occurred, an event that would wipe them from the face of the planet. What precisely transpired, and how? Let`s delve into this mystery.

"As it draws nearer to our planet, Earth's gravitational pull grows stronger," rendering its impending arrival invisible to those on the surface.

Ladies and gentlemen, the term 'Dinosaur' finds its origins in the Greek language, stemming from the words 'Denios,' meaning 'Terrible,' and 'Sauros,' meaning 'Lizard' – quite literally, 'Terrible Lizard.' This term first graced the pages of history in 1841 when the first dinosaur fossils were unearthed. A British scientist by the name of Richard Owen was the one who introduced the word 'dinosaur.' At the time, people possessed limited knowledge of these ancient creatures and their appearances. Consequently, the initial depictions of dinosaurs bore little resemblance to our contemporary understanding.

One of the earliest discovered fossils was that of the Megalosaurus, and when you examine the initial illustrations, they differ significantly from the images we have today. Over subsequent decades, as researchers uncovered more information about dinosaurs, these depictions were refined to portray a more realistic image. Today, over 10,000 dinosaur fossils have been excavated by paleontologists across the globe, leading to the identification of over

900 distinct species. It's truly exciting to think about the prospect of discovering more fossils.

Interestingly, from 2003 to 2022, an average of 45 new dinosaur species have been identified each year. This demonstrates that the work of paleontologists is far from complete. In fact, consider the images of newly discovered dinosaur species from the past year. Among them is a rather peculiar dinosaur found in Chile, boasting a blade-like tail weapon and a beak for a mouth, aptly named Stegouros Elengassen.

As of today, our knowledge of dinosaurs is quite extensive. However, let's embark on our journey starting from the very beginning, millions of years ago. Scientists estimate that the first dinosaurs emerged approximately 230-240 million years ago, with the oldest dinosaur fossils discovered thus far dating back to 231.4 million years ago in Africa. During this era, Earth bore little resemblance to its current form. All the continents we recognize today – Asia, Africa, Australia, Europe – were conjoined into a single supercontinent known as Pangaea. Scientists believe that Pangaea's arrangement resembled the continents we know today. This was a time of arid, dry climates with minimal rainfall, labeled the Triassic Period and the dawn of dinosaur emergence.

During this epoch, the dinosaurs differed greatly from our preconceived notions. They were notably smaller in size, with the average dinosaur of that era measuring merely around 2 meters in length. For instance, the Eoraptor, a dinosaur from this period, is considered the ancestor of later dinosaurs. The dominant creatures of this era were enormous reptiles, some of which might be considered rather endearing, such as one believed to be the ancestor of all turtles.

However, Earth underwent significant transformations as it approached the end of the Triassic period, roughly 201 million years ago. The supercontinent Pangaea began to fragment, a process that, although I use the term "suddenly," took place over thousands of years in the grand timescale of millions of years. Fissures appeared in the supercontinent, accompanied by substantial volcanic eruptions along these fault lines. These eruptions unleashed a deluge of carbon dioxide and sulfur dioxide into the atmosphere, triggering severe global warming. The entry of sulfur dioxide and aerosols into the atmosphere blocked sunlight, leading to localized cooling. When carbon dioxide and sulfur dioxide mixed with water, the oceans' acidity levels increased, setting off rapid and drastic climate changes. The implications of these transformations made survival increasingly difficult for the species of the era.

Most of the reptiles and other species from that period were cold-blooded creatures, ill-equipped to cope with dramatic shifts in temperature. Dinosaurs, however, shared a similarity with humans in that they were warm-blooded, making them better suited to endure these climatic fluctuations. These volcanic eruptions and climatic shifts persisted for around 600,000 years, pushing most other species to the brink of extinction. As a result, the sole survivors on Earth were the dinosaurs, crocodiles, turtles, and early mammals. This cataclysmic event is known as the Triassic-Jurassic Extinction Event.

And so, the Triassic period drew to a close, and the Jurassic period dawned. For those who might find the name familiar, it was the inspiration behind the famous "Jurassic Park" films. The term "Jurassic" is a reference to this specific period. The Jurassic period spanned from approximately 201 million to 145 million years ago. During this era, dinosaurs ascended to become the dominant species on the planet. Through the course of evolution, some grew to impressive sizes. For example, some of the early Titanosaurs, inhabitants of this period around 160 million years ago, could weigh up to a colossal 15,000 kilograms and measure up to 15 meters in length.

The Jurassic period also marked the emergence of dinosaurs capable of flight, exemplified by Archaeopteryx, one of the earliest feathered dinosaurs, which bore a resemblance to the birds we see today. During this period, Pangaea began its division into two smaller supercontinents: Laurasia and Gondwanaland. This period has gained notoriety thanks to the "Jurassic Park" films. However, the subsequent era, the Cretaceous period, bore witness to the true flourishing of the dinosaurs.

The Cretaceous period was particularly prolific, leading to a surge in the diversity of dinosaur species. This was the era when we encountered some of the most iconic dinosaurs, including the ever-famous Tyrannosaurus rex (T-Rex), which thrived towards the conclusion of the Cretaceous period, around 65-68 million years ago. Although there is some debate among researchers, most believe that T-Rex did not exist during the Jurassic period. It is intriguing to note the irony that the "Jurassic Park" film series used the T-Rex as its logo. The Cretaceous period stood as the longest epoch in the age of dinosaurs, commencing around 145 million years ago and concluding approximately 65 million years ago.

During this epoch, the two supercontinents, Laurasia and Gondwanaland, began to break apart, gradually shaping the continents into forms that resemble what we see on the world map today. The Cretaceous period was a time when numerous new species of dinosaurs emerged, including raptors, armored dinosaurs, giant herbivores, and formidable carnivores. Among them, the Titanosaurs, such as the Argentinosaurus, could weigh up to a staggering 77 tonnes.

This period also saw the development of numerous flowering plants, and Earth's climate was notably warmer. Sea levels rose, and almost every kind of dinosaur one can imagine proliferated.

Inhabiting this era were various dinosaurs, including raptors, armored dinosaurs, enormous herbivores, and formidable carnivores. Among them, the Titanosaurus stood as one of the largest terrestrial creatures ever known, while the Argentinosaurus could weigh up to a staggering 77 tonnes. The iconic T-Rex, believed to be the apex predator of its time, reached lengths of up to 40 feet and possessed the most powerful jaws of any known animal. Notably, the evolution of grass, which we commonly associate with Earth, commenced a mere 70 million years ago. Therefore, when envisioning the Earth in the narrative I've been sharing, it's important not to picture a world covered in grass; other plant varieties existed.

Around 68 million years ago, both the T-Rex and Triceratops evolved, marking a notable point in history. It's intriguing to note that we are closer in time to the existence of the T-Rex than it was to the Jurassic Period, with a span of 80 million years separating the two, whereas only 68 million years stand between us and the T-Rex.

Another intriguing species of dinosaurs that existed at the time were the Ornithomimids, which bore a resemblance to ostriches and ranked among the fastest dinosaurs, capable of sprinting at speeds of up to 80 km/hr. In terms of flight, the Quetzalcoatlus reigned as the largest flying dinosaur, boasting an impressive wingspan measuring 10-11 meters. This was indeed a prosperous era for dinosaurs, with the climate favoring their existence and the evolution of new species taking place. Furthermore, there was no other species to compete with them, allowing them to rule over Earth effortlessly.

However, this golden age came to an abrupt end when a colossal asteroid, measuring approximately 10-15 kilometers in diameter, hurtled towards Earth and collided with it 66 million years ago. The asteroid was traveling at an astounding speed of 30 kilometers per second, equivalent to 150 times the velocity of a jet airliner. Specifically, it struck the Yucatan Peninsula in Mexico, the same region that would later give rise to the Mayan civilization and historic wonders such as Chichen Itza.

The impact of the asteroid generated a massive crater with a diameter of 180 kilometers, releasing energy at an astonishing rate, equivalent to 100 teratonnes of TNT, which is a staggering 1 billion times the energy produced by the atomic bombs dropped on Hiroshima and Nagasaki. The impact led to the disintegration of everything within its vicinity. The impact expelled vast amounts of soil into the atmosphere, heating the land and causing scorching dust to rain down across distant areas.

Global temperatures skyrocketed by several degrees for hours, causing the incineration of all creatures within thousands of kilometers. It is believed that only small animals survived the initial blast by taking refuge underground, in water, caves, or within large tree trunks.

Nevertheless, the initial impact was just the beginning. Subsequent shock waves, heat pulses, wildfires spanning thousands of kilometers of forest, and enormous tsunamis ensued. It's conjectured that an immediate tsunami, with waves towering to 2 kilometers in height, struck the shores.

Can you fathom the sheer magnitude of a 2-kilometer-tall tsunami wave?

Volcanic eruptions rekindled, acid rain fell, and earthquakes rocked the Earth. The immediate consequences were exceptionally lethal. You might think that on the opposite side of the Earth, where the impact didn't reach, some animals could have survived. However, the long-term repercussions were even more deadly.

The fine dust particles thrown into the atmosphere blocked sunlight for the following year worldwide, triggering a nuclear winter. Temperatures plummeted dramatically, and for an estimated three years, Earth was encased in a deep freeze. This calamity killed numerous plants and animals as the absence of sunlight prevented photosynthesis. Plants withered, depriving herbivorous creatures of sustenance, and ultimately, even carnivorous animals starved due to the absence of prey. This chain reaction unraveled, and only small omnivorous creatures such as mammals, lizards, turtles, and some birds managed to endure by scavenging on dead dinosaurs, decaying plants, and fungi. This led to the release of carbon and sulfur into the atmosphere, causing sunlight to be significantly diminished for several thousand years.

And it didn't stop there; acid rain continued for thousands of years. Once the nuclear winter came to an end, the dust settled, and sunlight graced the Earth again. However, a significant amount of carbon dioxide had already been released into the atmosphere, resulting in intense global warming. Consider this, my friends – a single asteroid altered Earth's history for thousands of years.

With a few exceptions aside, no terrestrial four-legged creatures weighing over 25 kilograms managed to survive this catastrophic event. All terrestrial dinosaurs were wiped out, along with the plant and animal species that had once thrived on Earth. Over 75% of species faced extinction.

At this juncture, the Cretaceous period concluded, giving way to the Paleogene period. But it wasn't the end; instead, this event presented an opportunity for other animal species to rise. The dinosaurs, Earth's rulers, were no more, paving the way for the evolution of mammals in the wake of the dinosaurs' extinction.

Mammals stepped in to fill the ecological void left by the dinosaurs, and it was during this period that the evolution of horses, whales, bats, and primates occurred. The Paleogene era also saw the emergence of several snakes and smaller lizards. Remarkably, the only group of dinosaurs to survive were the flying dinosaurs, which gradually evolved into the birds we recognize today. That's right, the birds you observe soaring through the skies today share ancestry with these flying dinosaurs, most closely linked to chickens and ostriches.

This genetic relationship between birds and dinosaurs is supported by numerous studies. Indeed, the closest living relative of the fearsome T-Rex is believed to be a chicken, illustrating the fascinating connection between birds and these prehistoric creatures. As for the asteroid's impact site and the dating of this cataclysmic event, these details are supported by the presence of a rare mineral – iridium. Scientists have identified deposits of iridium at select locations on Earth, offering evidence of the asteroid strike and its occurrence approximately 66 million years ago.

A high concentration of iridium is found on Earth's surface, which is indeed a rare mineral within the Earth's composition. This anomaly is explained by the fact that comets and asteroids, bearing a substantial iridium content, are responsible for this occurrence. When scientists subjected the iridium layer to carbon dating, they determined that it dates back to 66 million years ago, marking the period of the asteroid impact that dispersed this mineral across the planet.

Despite the immense impact of the asteroid, you might wonder why the crater it left isn't more visible. However, the passage of 66 million years has caused considerable alterations in the Earth's geography due to the relentless movement of continents. The asteroid's crater is concealed within the Yucatan Peninsula, where numerous excavation expeditions have confirmed the event's actual occurrence and the precise location.

The crater's position is clearly marked on the map, with one half submerged beneath the sea and the other half on land. This impact's real-world manifestation can be observed in the cenotes of the Mexican region. These picturesque sinkholes exhibit a distinct pattern, forming a ring around the asteroid's crater. These cenotes have evolved into popular tourist attractions where visitors can partake in swimming activities. Collectively, these cenotes form the world's most extensive underground cave system.

When contemplating the ramifications of a current asteroid impact, it's reasonable to question if it could result in human extinction. Indeed, such an event poses a legitimate threat. Near Earth Asteroids, or NEAs, are the class of asteroids that might impact Earth in the foreseeable future. Agencies like NASA diligently monitor and track these NEAs to calculate their trajectories and assess the potential for Earth impact.

As of April 2022, more than 28,000 NEAs have been identified, including over 800 with diameters of 1 kilometer or more, underscoring the potential hazard they pose. However, there's no need for immediate alarm because scientific advancements enable the precise prediction of their paths and the estimation of the probability of impact. Furthermore, strategies are in place to mitigate potential threats, as demonstrated by NASA's DART space mission, launched in 2021 (Double Asteroid Redirection Test). This mission entailed colliding a spacecraft with an asteroid to alter its trajectory. The success of this test on an asteroid not on a collision course with Earth highlights the feasibility of such efforts if an asteroid were to threaten Earth in the future.

Nonetheless, the danger of asteroid impact isn't the only peril humanity faces. The asteroid strike that extinguished the dinosaurs is categorized as the fifth mass extinction event in Earth's history. However, scientists believe that the sixth mass extinction event has already commenced, and it is driven by human activities.

This ongoing event is known as the Holocene Extinction Event. Over the last 100-200 years, human-induced factors, such as deforestation and pollution of the oceans and atmosphere, have precipitated an unprecedented loss of biodiversity. Biologists concur that this constitutes a mass extinction event with the extinction rate exceeding the natural rate by more than 100 to 1,000 times.

Human actions have disrupted the habitats of many species, pushing thousands of mammals, birds, reptiles, and amphibians into the endangered category or causing their outright extinction. To combat this devastation, a United Nations Convention on Biological Diversity Meeting was convened in Japan in 2010, where 20 biodiversity targets were established with a deadline of 2020. Unfortunately, only six of these targets were partially met. In January 2020, a new initiative, akin to the Paris Agreement, was launched to prevent biodiversity and ecosystem collapse, setting a deadline for 2030. Its objectives include designating 30% of land and oceans as protected areas and reducing pollution by at least 50%. Scientists have suggested that the ongoing extinctions must be limited to 20 or fewer species per year.

The ultimate success of these endeavors remains to be seen, but they are critically important. If plant and animal species continue to go extinct as they have in previous extinction events, it may become impossible for humans to survive. Intriguingly, humans, as per scientific estimations, emerged a mere 300,000 years ago in Africa. This is in stark contrast to the reign of the dinosaurs, which persisted as Earth's dominant species for an astounding 174 million years. Humans, by comparison, have been present for only 300,000 years, which is merely 600 times shorter than the reign of the dinosaurs.

Whether humans can surpass the record set by dinosaurs or face extinction before reaching one million years depends largely on collective efforts to preserve the planet. The right answer hinges on these collective endeavors.

7. Mona Lisa Unveiled: The World's Most Famous Painting

On the 21st of August 1911, a bustling Monday morning in the vibrant city of Paris, something extraordinary occurred. As office-goers hurried to their workplaces, three mysterious figures emerged from the hallowed halls of the Louvre Museum. These three individuals had spent the previous night concealed within the museum's walls, and now they were making a hasty exit, carrying an invaluable item from the Louvre, hidden beneath a nondescript blanket. Their destination? A nearby railway station, where they boarded a train at precisely 8:45 in the morning, vanishing into obscurity. Little did the world know that a heist of one of the most renowned paintings in history had just taken place – the enigmatic and iconic Mona Lisa.

Today, the Mona Lisa is valued at nearly $1 billion, but what is the secret to its unparalleled fame? What mysteries are concealed within this remarkable work of art? To comprehend the allure of the Mona Lisa, we must first explore the life of the mastermind behind it – the extraordinary Italian artist, scientist, and polymath, Leonardo da Vinci.

Leonardo da Vinci's genius extended far beyond painting. He was a visionary, an engineer, a scientist, a sculptor, an architect, and a theorist. His vast knowledge spanned a multitude of disciplines, including painting, cartography, astronomy, anatomy, botany, hydrology, geology, optics, and even paleontology. A detailed exploration of his life would be an adventure in itself, but for now, let's focus on his most celebrated creation – the Mona Lisa.

One of the enduring mysteries surrounding the Mona Lisa is the identity of the woman depicted in the painting. The first revelation regarding her identity came from Italian artist Giorgio Vasari, who, in 1550, penned an autobiography of Leonardo da Vinci. According to Vasari, the woman was Lisa Gherardini, who was married to Francesco Giocondo, a silk trader from Florence. Vasari suggested that Francesco had commissioned the painting of his wife, providing the origins of the painting's names. The name "Mona Lisa" is derived from "Madonna

Lisa," with "Madonna" traditionally signifying "Madam" in Italian. "Madonna Lisa" eventually evolved into "Monna Lisa" in Italian, and when this was anglicized, "Mona Lisa" emerged as the famous appellation. Additionally, she is known as "La Gioconda," signifying "joyful" or "light-hearted" in Italian, which was an apt a of Lisa Gherardini's disposition. This name was adopted in France as "La Joconde." Despite Vasari's disclosure, there were numerous theories and speculations regarding the woman's identity. Some suggested that the painting was a portrayal of Leonardo da Vinci's mother, a queen from Italian aristocracy, or even a self-portrait of Da Vinci in the guise of a woman. The latter theory, suggesting that the Mona Lisa was not a woman at all, persisted for a while, but modern research has provided substantial evidence confirming that the woman in the painting is indeed Lisa Gherardini. A Florence-based professor conducted extensive research for 25 years, unearthing archives and evidence that solidified Lisa's identity and the connections between her family and the da Vinci family. It is likely that the painting was not commissioned by Lisa's husband but by Leonardo's father.

Furthermore, Mona Lisa's age is a subject of intrigue. When the painting was created in 1503, Lisa Gherardini was approximately 24 years old. The timing of the painting is speculated to be linked to either Lisa and Francesco's purchase of a home in 1503 or the birth of their second son in December 1502. The latter seems more plausible, particularly considering the tragic loss of Lisa's daughter in 1499. An intriguing detail in the painting is the veil covering Lisa's hair, which some interpret as a mourning veil worn by those who have experienced a family loss.

So, why is the Mona Lisa, an Italian masterpiece, displayed in France? This can be attributed to an invitation extended to Leonardo da Vinci by King Francis I of France in 1516. Leonardo decided to leave Italy and relocated to France, taking the Mona Lisa with him. Although historical records are somewhat ambiguous, it is believed that he had not completed the painting by that time.

One of the most captivating aspects of the Mona Lisa is its enigmatic smile, which has intrigued observers for centuries. To achieve this subtle, mysterious expression, da Vinci employed a unique painting style known as "Sfumato," which involves skillful blending. The background of the painting, depicting the Arno Valley in Italy, seamlessly melds with the image of Mona Lisa. This technique, which blurs boundaries and features a seamless blending of colors, creates the impression that there are no clear outlines between the background and the subject. It is this meticulous attention to detail that brings the Mona Lisa's smile to life. When closely examined, her smile may appear enigmatic and almost flat. However, when observed from a peripheral view, her smile seems to subtly change. This effect is due to da Vinci's unparalleled understanding of facial muscles, light, and shadow. In fact, he spent extensive time dissecting facial muscles, even resorting to studying horses for comparison, all to perfect the Mona Lisa's smile.

But here's a fascinating revelation: there isn't just one Mona Lisa; there are two. The story of the second Mona Lisa began in 1504 when another renowned artist, Raphael, created a preliminary sketch. This sketch significantly differs from the Mona Lisa in the Louvre, featuring two columns in the background. Initially, it was believed that Raphael had based his drawing on the Mona Lisa painting. However, in 1993, a German art historian disproved this theory. Instead, it was discovered that Raphael lived across from the Giocondo family in Florence, possibly indicating that another Mona Lisa served as the inspiration for Raphael's drawing. In 1914, a novelist residing near London, John R. Eyre, introduced a new version of the Mona Lisa, which aligned with Raphael's drawing. This "second" Mona Lisa is distinct from the one displayed at the Louvre. It presents a younger-looking subject, a slightly tilted head, and a more straightforward and unambiguous expression, devoid of the enigmatic smile. This discovery has led to a theory suggesting that Leonardo da Vinci worked on two versions of the Mona Lisa. The Isleworth Mona Lisa, which was discovered later, is considered to be the first iteration, reflecting da Vinci's experimental style during the painting's early stages.

As for the theft of the Mona Lisa, it was orchestrated by Vincenzo Peruggia, an employee at the Louvre Museum. He concealed himself within the museum overnight, then made off with the painting in the morning. Peruggia believed that, as an Italian creation, the Mona Lisa should be returned to Italy. The audacious theft grabbed global headlines, and detectives were deployed in search of the elusive thief. However, Peruggia successfully concealed the painting for two years, pondering his next move. He ultimately attempted to sell the artwork in Florence to art dealer Giovanni Poggi. Suspicion arose, and when Poggi examined the painting's stamp, he made a stunning discovery — he was in possession of the most sought-after item in the world. Vincenzo was apprehended, and the Mona Lisa was restored to

the Louvre. Today, the painting is showcased behind bulletproof glass in a climate-controlled environment with precise humidity and temperature controls.

Curiously, the theft of the Mona Lisa inadvertently contributed to its rise in global popularity. Before the theft, it was not as widely known among the general public. It was only afterward that the Mona Lisa became a symbol of art and intrigue, attracting visitors from around the world.

In conclusion, the Mona Lisa remains an enigmatic masterpiece, attributed to the genius of Leonardo da Vinci and shrouded in mystery regarding its subject, Lisa Gherardini. This iconic painting, with its timeless allure, continues to captivate the world and is celebrated for its artistry and the secrets hidden within its subtle details.

Fifteen years elapsed since the commencement of the painting, during which Leonardo da Vinci relentlessly worked to enhance and perfect it. However, in the year 1519, the world lost the brilliant artist when he passed away while residing in the French palace. The painting remained in the possession of the king and became a cherished part of his Royal Collection.

Approximately 150 years later, in 1797, a significant historical event, the French Revolution, unfolded. This tumultuous period saw the Mona Lisa removed from the royal palace and placed under the care of the Louvre Museum, where it resides to this day.

An intriguing detail lies at the heart of the Mona Lisa's history: the painting's theft in 1911. I discussed this event at the outset of our exploration. Vincenzo Peruggia, an Italian Nationalist, masterminded this audacious heist, carried out with the assistance of two accomplices. Peruggia's motivation was rooted in his belief that the Mona Lisa rightfully belonged to Italy, not France. Following the theft, they transported the painting to Italy, a daring endeavor, particularly considering the artwork's immense value, reaching into the millions of dollars. Predictably, Vincenzo could not have felt secure after orchestrating such a high-stakes theft.

Now, let's return to the narrative of Vincenzo, the Italian nationalist, and explore the events that followed. But before delving into that, let's delve into the distinctive characteristics that make the Mona Lisa a work of unparalleled significance.

Firstly, the Mona Lisa is not rendered on paper, canvas, or fabric, as is customary for paintings. Instead, Leonardo da Vinci employed poplar wood as the canvas. During the era in which he created this masterpiece, poplar wood was the favored medium of Italian painters.

Secondly, the painting is relatively small in size, as exemplified by photographs that depict its placement in the museum. The dimensions of the Mona Lisa are a mere 77 cm by 53 cm. Despite its modest proportions, it holds an extraordinary distinction: it was among the first paintings in Italy of its time to feature an incredibly detailed and close-up portrayal of an individual. This constitutes a half-length portrait, a style akin to contemporary portrait photography but unconventional for its era.

A notable aspect of the Mona Lisa's visual composition is its predominant use of brown and yellow hues, resulting in a somewhat subdued appearance. It exhibits a peculiarly yellowish tone, which, at one point, led a professor to speculate that Lisa depicted a patient with high cholesterol. This coloration can be attributed to two factors. Firstly, a protective varnish was applied to shield the painting from the harmful effects of humidity and moisture, considering its wooden canvas. Secondly, the passage of time led to a gradual bleaching effect, causing the painting to lose some of its original vibrancy.

To further grasp the Mona Lisa's magnetic quality, it is crucial to understand Leonardo da Vinci's innovative painting technique known as "Sfumato," which hinges on masterful blending. The painting's background, featuring the picturesque Arno Valley in Italy, seamlessly merges with the image of the Mona Lisa. Da Vinci's approach eliminates clear boundaries between the background and the subject, with instances where Mona Lisa's hair blends harmoniously with the landscape. The blurred lines and melded colors epitomize the Sfumato technique and play a pivotal role in creating the enigmatic smile that has intrigued countless observers. If you closely scrutinize Mona Lisa's smile, you may find it appears quite serious upon detailed inspection. Yet, when you shift your focus to her eyes, the smile appears to subtly intensify. This optical illusion arises from the meticulous application of the Sfumato technique, underpinned by da Vinci's deep understanding of facial muscles, light, and shadow.

Leonardo da Vinci's relentless pursuit of perfection extended to the study of human anatomy, particularly the facial muscles and nerves responsible for crafting a smile. He spent many nights dissecting cadavers in a Florence hospital to unravel the secrets of the human smile, emphasizing the multitude of muscles in the human lip area. In his notes, he recorded that "the muscles which move the lips are more numerous in man than in any other animal." Dissecting these intricate facial muscles was a formidable task due to their small size and multiplicity. To gain deeper insights, da Vinci even examined horses, comparing their facial expressions to those of humans. His obsession with perfecting the Mona Lisa's smile went to the extent of delving into optics. He deduced that light rays do not converge into a single point on the human retina, instead dispersing across its surface. The central region, known as the Fovea, is responsible for processing fine details, while the surrounding areas are attuned to shadows and black-and-white imagery. Armed with this knowledge, he subtly adjusted the shadows in such a way that even when you view the Mona Lisa in your peripheral vision, her smile continues to have an effect. The central line of her smile appears relatively flat when observed up close, thus creating the impression of a neutral expression. However, when considering the shadows applied using the Sfumato technique, they evoke a smile perception when viewed peripherally.

Unveiling a captivating revelation, it is not a single Mona Lisa but two. This revelation is grounded in historical fact rather than conspiracy theory. The story of the second Mona Lisa commenced in 1504 when another renowned artist, Raphael, created a preliminary sketch with pen and ink. This sketch significantly diverged from the well-known Mona Lisa displayed at the Louvre. The crucial distinction was the presence of two columns in the background of Raphael's sketch, deviating from the conventional Mona Lisa's background. The insightful work of a German art historian in 1993 discredited the notion that Raphael had based his drawing on the original Mona Lisa. Instead, it was established that Raphael had lived across from the Giocondo family in Florence, potentially inspiring the drawing. It was only in 1914 that a writer residing near London, John R. Eyre, introduced another rendition of the Mona Lisa, aligning with Raphael's drawing. Termed the "Isleworth Mona Lisa," this distinct version presents a younger, differently posed subject with a more straightforward, unambiguous expression, devoid of the iconic enigmatic smile. This discovery has led to a compelling theory suggesting that Leonardo da Vinci may have worked on two versions of the Mona Lisa, with the Isleworth Mona Lisa representing an earlier stage in the painting's evolution.

In summary, the Mona Lisa is an enduring masterpiece, attributed to the genius of Leonardo da Vinci and veiled in the mystery surrounding its subject, Lisa Gherardini. This iconic painting, with its timeless appeal, continues to captivate the world and is celebrated for its artistry and the secrets concealed within its subtle intricacies.

A striking disparity becomes evident when we examine Raphael's sketch alongside the Mona Lisa. Notably, Raphael's sketch features two columns situated behind Mona Lisa, initially prompting the belief that Raphael had fashioned his drawing based on the Mona Lisa painting. Nevertheless, this assumption was dispelled by a German art historian in 1993. Professor Pallanti, the dedicated researcher whose work I previously mentioned, offered a compelling revelation. He unearthed evidence that Raphael had resided directly opposite the Giocondo family in Florence. This raises an astonishing possibility: Did Raphael create an entirely distinct painting on the same subject, with the same woman and identical pose? The prospect seems almost incredulous.

However, an alternative explanation emerges, suggesting the existence of another Mona Lisa painting that inspired Raphael's drawing. This second Mona Lisa came to light in 1914 through the efforts of John R. Eyre, a novelist residing in the vicinity of London. Eyre introduced a new rendition of the Mona Lisa, which served as the basis for Raphael's sketch. This second Mona Lisa diverges from the Louvre's iconic version in several aspects. Firstly, the woman portrayed in this newly discovered version appears notably younger. Secondly, the positioning of her head tilts slightly forward, creating a nuanced difference. Most conspicuously, the expressions exhibited by this new Mona Lisa are unequivocal and devoid of the enigmatic smile that characterizes the Louvre's Mona Lisa. The two columns in the background align with those seen in Raphael's drawing.

Consequently, experts put forth a theory that Leonardo da Vinci may have been working on two distinct renditions of the Mona Lisa. Both of these paintings are attributed to da Vinci's hand. The Isleworth Mona Lisa, unveiled later, is considered the initial version of da Vinci's work, reflecting an experimental phase where the subject appears more youthful than in the other painting. Nonetheless, it's important to note that this theory remains a subject of ongoing debate, and no definitive evidence has conclusively validated either perspective.

Shifting our focus back to the theft of the Mona Lisa, an astonishing revelation came to light. The mastermind behind this audacious theft was none other than Vincenzo Peruggia, an employee at the Louvre Museum. He ingeniously concealed himself within the museum one night, later emerging in the morning with the painting in his possession. Peruggia firmly believed that this masterpiece, created by the Italian Leonardo da Vinci, rightfully belonged in an Italian museum. Upon news of the theft spreading worldwide, the heist became a sensation, captivating the global media. In response, numerous detectives embarked on a relentless quest to apprehend the thief, but their efforts proved futile.

Peruggia maintained the painting in secrecy within his home for a duration of two years, pondering his next course of action. Growing impatient and contemplating how to profit from this immensely sought-after artwork, he attempted to sell it to an art dealer in Florence, Giovanni Poggi. Upon closer inspection, Giovanni Poggi grew suspicious and verified the painting's authenticity using a stamp, confirming that it was, indeed, the stolen masterpiece. Vincenzo Peruggia's audacious act ultimately led to his capture and a subsequent six-month prison sentence.

The painting was subsequently returned to its rightful place at the Louvre Museum and restored on January 4, 1914. Today, it is displayed within the museum behind bulletproof glass and under meticulously controlled environmental conditions. The climate is rigorously maintained at 50% humidity with a temperature range between 18°C to 21°C.

Ironically, one of the most fascinating aspects of this narrative is that the Mona Lisa's widespread recognition and fame commenced in earnest only after its theft. Before this infamous incident, the Mona Lisa was not particularly renowned among the general public. While art enthusiasts were familiar with it, the painting had not achieved the global recognition it enjoys today. Consequently, when you visit the Louvre Museum and witness the bustling crowds surrounding the

Mona Lisa, you can attribute this surge in popularity to the audacity of Vincenzo Peruggia.

8. Secrets of Area 51: Fact or Fiction?

In July of 1947, there was a widespread UFO craze in America. Reports of UFO sightings, or unidentified flying objects, were pouring in from all over the country. The excitement began in late June when a private pilot named Kenneth Arnold claimed he had seen nine shining UFOs near a hill in the vicinity of Seattle. According to Arnold, these UFOs were zipping through the skies at incredible speeds, clocking in at 2,000 kilometers per hour. In just two weeks, people from various parts of America reported their own encounters with flying UFOs. The media was abuzz with discussions about these sightings.

This map illustrates the locations of these UFO sightings across America. The media began linking the UFO phenomena to atomic sites and focused on three specific areas with the highest number of sightings, which were coincidentally near nuclear test sites. Meanwhile, in New Mexico, a man named Mac Brazel found unusual debris on his field. This debris consisted of tin foil, rubber, and a thin wooden beam. Perplexed by what he had discovered, Brazel wondered if this debris might be connected to the ongoing UFO craze. He decided to take the material to the Roswell Sheriff's office on July 7th.

This act caught the attention of Colonel William Blanchard, who was the commanding officer of the Roswell Army Airfield (RAAF). The following day, RAAF issued a statement, confirming the rumors of "flying disks." They stated, "The 509th Bomb Group of the 8th Airforce, Roswell Army Airfield was fortunate enough to gain possession of a disk." The U.S. Army's announcement seemed to provide proof of UFOs' existence.

However, the very next day, the U.S. Army officials retracted their stance. They claimed that the debris they received was from a weather balloon. As evidence, they released photographs of Major Marcel with the alleged weather balloon debris. With that, the news surrounding the UFOs died down, and both the media and the public lost interest.

Years later, in the late 1970s, rumors resurfaced regarding an alien craft spotted flying over the New Mexico desert. These rumors suggested that the UFO had crashed after being struck by lightning, resulting in the deaths of the extraterrestrial beings on board. In 1980, Major Marcel authored a book titled 'The Roswell Incident,' in which he claimed that the debris he had seen was "not made on this Earth" and appeared to be of extraterrestrial origin.

Since then, the significance of the Roswell Incident continued to grow. New theories emerged, with some individuals asserting that a live alien was discovered at the crash site, and the U.S. Army had kept it hidden at a top-secret facility. Some believed that the alien was still imprisoned in this secret location, and the U.S. Army was engaged in reverse-engineering alien technology and conducting research on extraterrestrial life.

All of these activities were said to be taking place at a top-secret facility, famously known as Area 51. To unravel this mystery, let's delve into this intriguing tale.

"Since the late 1940s, Americans have been captivated by a mysterious region in Nevada, known as Area 51. But what exactly goes on at Area 51? The Air Force has recently made public an archive of UFO reports and investigations, leading to questions like: Are there any alien remains in Area 51?

Area 51 is a highly secretive U.S. military facility situated in the midst of a desolate desert, miles away from the nearest cities. Access to this facility, along with any attempts to trespass or enter it, is strictly prohibited. Warning signs are prevalent in the area, cautioning against photography and emphasizing that any suspicious activity would be met with deadly force.

Now, you might wonder, what's inside Area 51? In recent years, it has gained notoriety thanks to an interesting incident. In June 2019, Joe Rogan, a well-known podcaster, invited Bob Lazar, a cult figure with a penchant for UFOs, to discuss his beliefs and experiences regarding UFOs. Lazar claimed to have conducted extensive research on flying saucers and Area 51, asserting that he had been employed as a researcher within Area 51. His purported role was to investigate alien technology, reverse-engineer it, and enhance our modern technology through these discoveries.

Lazar stated, "This project was to back-engineer the alien craft. I went through the hangar door, and inside the hangar door was the disk, the flying saucer that I worked on." This podcast interview had a significant impact.

Subsequently, a college student named Matty Roberts was inspired by this podcast and wanted to uncover the government's hidden secrets. He understood that individual efforts to discover the truth might be thwarted and silenced by the government. However, he believed that if a large crowd gathered at Area 51, the government would be unable to prevent them from infiltrating the top-secret facility. Thus, he created a Facebook event named 'Storm Area 51, They Can't Stop All Of Us.'

In this event, Roberts suggested that people assemble at Area 51 at 3 AM on September 20, 2019, to coordinate and attempt to penetrate the clandestine facility. The event was initially intended as a humorous prank and included eccentric elements like the 'Naruto Run.' According to the event post, the 'Naruto Run' would help participants evade bullets if the military attempted to open fire. This run is inspired by the Japanese manga series 'Naruto,' in which the main character runs with a distinctive posture.

Surprisingly, this prank event gained significant traction and drew the attention of more than 2 million people who confirmed their intention to participate in the event. Matty Roberts, realizing that his joke had spiraled into a massive phenomenon, expressed his concerns about the situation. In his statement, he absolved himself of responsibility, explicitly stating that he was not accountable for the actions of the two million individuals who expressed an interest in the event.

However, actually getting to Area 51 was not a straightforward task for those who wanted to attend. Area 51 is located in the heart of a desert, miles away from any significant cities or infrastructure. The area is exceptionally isolated, with only a 250-kilometer-long highway passing through the desert, devoid of any gas stations. The summer mornings in this region can be scorching, with temperatures exceeding 40°C. The only nearby settlement, Rachel, was reported to have a population of just 54 residents in 2019.

The isolation of this area is due to the fact that Area 51 is situated within the Nevada Test and Training Range, the largest government-controlled land in the United States.

This vast area covers more than 12,000 square kilometers. Adjacent to this facility lies another highly restricted military base, the Nevada Test Site, which was historically used for testing nuclear weapons from the 1950s through the 1990s. It is understandable that a site where nuclear weapons were detonated must be kept under strict control for safety and security reasons.

Before delving further into this event, it's essential to comprehend the history of Area 51, which is intertwined with the context of the Cold War. Area 51 was established during the Cold War, a period marked by intense competition and tension between the United States and the Soviet Union.

At the time, concerns were growing about communist infiltration within unions, the entertainment industry, and even the military and government. Area 51 was established to serve as a secretive testing and development facility for aircraft. During the 1950s, this facility played a pivotal role in testing some of the most critical espionage aircraft in American history. The importance of these military weapons' development led to the tight secrecy surrounding the facility.

In 1954, President Dwight D. Eisenhower of the United States mandated the creation of a classified location to initiate the High-Altitude Reconnaissance Program, a project aimed at developing spy planes capable of countering the Soviet Union's nuclear capabilities. Two CIA officers were assigned the task of identifying a suitable location to conduct tests and research for the development of spy planes that could prove effective against the Soviet Union's nuclear arsenal.

According to Annie Jacobsen's book, 'Area 51: An Uncensored History of America's Top Secret Military Base,' this secret facility was discovered in the midst of a desiccated lake bed in Nevada, originally known as Groom Lake. It later became synonymous with Area 51. The site was already designated as a classified area, where the government had been conducting tests related to nuclear weapons.

Area 51 served as a hub for the development of spy aircraft, particularly notable were two aircraft models. The U-2 Spy plane, which possessed a distinctive appearance, became an integral part of American espionage during the Cold War. The absence of satellite technology made it almost impossible for the United States to gather information about the Soviet Union's activities, especially following their successful testing of an atomic bomb in 1949. As a response, in 1953, President Eisenhower launched a covert CIA program named 'Project Aquatone,' designed to construct an aircraft with a $22 million budget that could travel 4,800 kilometers without refueling. This aircraft was equipped to carry a 320-kilogram payload of cameras while flying at an altitude of 21,000 meters. It was engineered to be undetectable on radar and impervious to anti-aircraft missiles.

This initiative gave rise to the U-2 spy plane, a pivotal asset in American espionage history, enabling them to gather critical intelligence on the Soviet Union. However, the triumph was short-lived as a U-2 aircraft was shot down by a missile on May 1, 1960. This incident compromised years of hard-won secrecy for the U.S. intelligence community. The United States was compelled to admit its spying activities. Consequently, the military was pressurized by the government to develop an aircraft that was not susceptible to such downing, capable of greater speed, and even more covert. This marked the birth of the Lockheed SR-71 Blackbird, which remains the fastest aircraft to this day, boasting a top speed of 3,400 kilometers per hour and an operating altitude of 24,000 meters. Its exceptional speed and altitude made it impervious to interception.

Given the critical nature of this top-secret aircraft, maintaining its secrecy was paramount, especially during the ongoing Cold War. This begged the question of how the military could test such an advanced plane while keeping it hidden from the world. The CIA provided an ingenious solution by allowing UFO conspiracy theories to circulate. These unidentified aerial phenomena, as referred to by the U.S. Department of Defense, were neither confirmed nor denied by the CIA. The strange and rapid unidentified objects observed in the sky raised questions about the existence of alien flying saucers, providing a perfect cover for the CIA to carry out its classified program while keeping the public distracted. By fueling these UFO rumors, the CIA allowed people to believe they were encountering alien spacecraft, rather than realizing they were witnessing U.S. military aircraft.

This approach is believed to be the reason behind the promotion of the flying saucer theory in the Roswell Incident, which dominated the media and newspapers for a brief period. However, the CIA was well aware that if the government acknowledged the existence of aliens and their involvement in experiments on extraterrestrial beings, it could result in widespread fear and paranoia among the public.

As mentioned at the beginning of this chapter, the resurgence of UFO rumors in the 1970s can be attributed to the testing of the Blackbird SR-71 aircraft during that period.

In 1994, we finally uncovered the factual events surrounding a legendary pilot embarking on the first-ever flight in a legendary aircraft. However, despite the availability of these facts, certain individuals continued to perpetuate conspiracy theories linking Area 51 to extraterrestrial beings. One notable figure in this regard is Bob Lazar. In 1989, he asserted that he had worked within Area 51's Sector

4 (S-4) and had been engaged in projects related to alien spacecraft on behalf of the government. Nevertheless, contemporary experts with credibility and neutrality have cast doubt on the veracity of his claims.

Now, let's explore what transpired with the event that attracted two million people. The security personnel responsible for overseeing Area 51 expected only 30,000 attendees out of the two million due to the site's extreme isolation and the difficulties involved in reaching it. The 'Storm Area 51' event gradually transformed into a music festival with an alien theme. Its organizer, Matty Roberts, began branding the event as 'Alienstock.' However, when the event day arrived, only 6,000 people turned up out of the projected 30,000. Most participants were aware that there were no significant nearby cities or infrastructure, so they brought their tents and set up camp.

On the government's side, there was substantial concern regarding the event, primarily stemming from the uncertainty about the number of attendees. Consequently, the number of law enforcement officers present at the event exceeded the actual number of attendees. Fortunately, the event transpired peacefully, characterized by enjoyment, festivities, and a notable absence of attempts to infiltrate Area 51. No damage was inflicted upon property. However, the sheriff reported that the high number of police officers deployed for security purposes incurred an estimated cost of $300,000.

Revisiting the Roswell incident, it is imperative to consider the official explanation presented by the military, wherein the debris was attributed to a weather balloon. It wasn't until 1994 that we discovered the genuine nature of the debris when the U.S. Air Force disclosed that it was associated with a nuclear surveillance balloon used in Project Mogul. The purpose of this balloon was to detect sound waves from distant nuclear tests conducted by the Soviet Union. The perpetuation of conspiracy theories can be partially attributed to the government's history of misleading statements. Consequently, even when they released the accurate explanation in

1994, public skepticism persisted due to diminished trust in government statements.

Nonetheless, it's crucial to emphasize that most UFO sightings can be attributed to misidentifications of various military objects such as drones, decoy flares, or unknown aircraft developments by the military. The term UFO denotes 'Unidentified Flying Objects,' with no assertion of extraterrestrial origins. Given the testing of unconventional-looking aircraft, including the U-2 and SR-71, around Area 51, it's understandable why this facility became associated with alien activities.

The U.S. Air Force's Project Blue Book was responsible for investigating numerous UFO sightings. Whenever individuals claimed to have observed UFOs, their reports were cross-referenced with flight records to determine the actual aircraft responsible for the sightings. This scrutiny led to the elimination of many UFO reports in the late 1950s and 1960s.

One key conspiracy theorist, Bob Lazar, claimed to have conducted government research on alien technology but was later revealed to have fabricated his educational background, including a fake degree from MIT. His claims about Element 115 as an alien spacecraft power source were debunked when Russian scientists produced the element and named it Moscovium in 2003.

In June 2013, the CIA officially recognized Area 51, declassifying the previously secret details surrounding its history under the Freedom of Information Act. In a similar manner to India's Right to Information Act (RTI), the U.S. employs the Freedom of Information Act for requesting government information. The government's acknowledgement of the base's existence, as well as the release of classified information, further demystified Area 51's secretive reputation. In addition, the CIA declassified around 13 million pages of documents in January 2017, many of which contained records related to UFO sightings and CIA experiments. They have continued to release information on UFOs or Unidentified Aerial Phenomena (UAP) in January 2021.

With these developments, the U.S. government has shifted away from the term 'UFO' to 'UAP,' which stands for 'Unidentified Aerial Phenomena,' to alleviate the heavy association of UFOs with aliens. In fact, the government has directed the release of information it possesses about UFOs and UAPs, reflecting a commitment to transparency and openness. In April 2020, the Pentagon released three videos that were leaked in 2007 and 2017, verifying their authenticity. In August 2020, a UAP Task Force was established by the Defense Department to detect, analyze, and catalog observed UAPs, which are perceived as potential national security threats.

It is important to acknowledge that not all UFOs or UAPs are identified. Recent years have witnessed multiple instances of U.S. military pilots encountering such phenomena, although they refrain from attributing them to extraterrestrial origins. The scrutiny surrounding these unidentified aerial phenomena persists, and Area 51 continues to serve as a site for testing next-generation aircraft.

Today, Area 51 has achieved global notoriety, attracting tourists from all over the world. In 1996, the state of Nevada renamed the highway leading to Area 51 as the 'Extraterrestrial Highway.' This decision was made to capitalize on the public's fascination with the conspiracy theory and promote tourism in the area. Despite its newfound popularity, Area 51 remains a military facility. Attempting to trespass into the base will result in arrest, as was demonstrated when a Dutch YouTuber, Ties Granzier, and others trespassed into Area 51, resulting in a three-day jail sentence.

9. Pyramids Revealed: Unmasking Their Construction

Approximately 4,500 years ago, a remarkable wonder was constructed in Egypt, one that continues to captivate people's imaginations even today – the Great Pyramid of Giza. Rising to a height of 147 meters, it held the title of the world's tallest structure for over 4,000 years. To create this monumental edifice, massive stones were employed, with an estimated total weight of 6 million tonnes. In contrast, the contemporary Burj Khalifa, the world's tallest building, weighs a mere 500,000 tonnes. The question that has left people awestruck for centuries is how this magnificent structure was constructed.

During that era, people lacked the modern machinery, cranes, and technology we possess today, and even wheels were not part of their toolkit. Yet, they managed to build a monument that endures to this day, standing tall for over 4,500 years, withstanding the elements such as harsh summers, storms, torrential rains, and the test of time. No other ancient structure has endured for as long or matched its scale. How was this remarkable feat accomplished?

"The Great Pyramid is arguably the most enigmatic structure on the face of the Earth. Built around 2,500 BC, it is the tallest structure on the Earth for more than 3,500 years. Built as gargantuan tombs of shining white limestone, the Pyramids are designed to hide the dark secrets of the dead."

As we venture further into the past, the task of deciphering precise events becomes increasingly challenging. The Great Pyramid of Giza is believed to have been constructed in 2560 BC, during the reign of Pharaoh Khufu. The Pharaohs ruled ancient Egypt, with Pharaoh Khufu belonging to the fourth dynasty of the Old Kingdom of Egypt. Much remains uncertain about Pharaoh Khufu's reign, with historians providing varying estimates for its duration, ranging from 23 to more than 60 years.

This remarkable pyramid, situated on the west bank of the River Nile, is not alone in its grandeur. When viewing Map, images or videos, you'll notice two other pyramids located nearby. Among these three, the tallest and most iconic is the Pyramid of Giza, also known as the Pyramid of Khufu. Slightly smaller is the Pyramid of Khafre, constructed by Khufu's son, Khafre. The third and smallest pyramid is the Pyramid of Menkaure, attributed to Khafre's son. Together with these pyramids, the site also encompasses the Great Sphinx, various burial tombs, and smaller pyramids. In total, there are approximately 118 pyramids of diverse shapes and sizes. Many of these structures have weathered over time, while only a few remain in relatively good condition. Notably, these three pyramids are among the best-preserved. It is important to understand the purpose behind their construction.

These pyramids were constructed for the same reason that prompted the creation of many ancient monuments: they were intended as tombs for the Pharaohs. Ancient Egyptians held strong beliefs in the afterlife, thinking that existence continued beyond death. According to their beliefs, the soul of a deceased individual embarked on a journey to the underworld, where it faced judgment by the Gods. Those who had lived virtuous lives were destined for immortality in the afterlife. To prepare for this journey, Pharaohs commissioned the construction of tombs while they reigned. These tombs were laden with substantial quantities of food, treasures, jewelry, furniture, clothing, and other items to facilitate their use in the afterlife. Following the Pharaoh's death, their bodies were mummified and then placed in a wooden or stone sarcophagus.

One may question the basis for this understanding. There are two primary reasons. First, inscriptions and texts have been discovered on various pyramids and sarcophagi, offering insights into the customs and rituals of the ancient Egyptians. Second, the majority of historical pyramids in Egypt and Sudan were used for burial purposes. However, it's essential to acknowledge that the Great Pyramid of Giza does not contain substantial evidence corroborating its function as a tomb, leading to alternative theories. Archaeologists entering the Great Pyramid found three relics and an empty sarcophagus, presumed to belong to Khufu. The treasures that originally surrounded the sarcophagus are thought to have been looted before archaeologists arrived at the site.

Individuals who dispute the tomb theory have put forth unusual alternative hypotheses. One prominent theory suggests that the Great Pyramid was a power plant capable of generating electricity. Proponents of this theory argue that ancient Egyptians possessed advanced technology, including the knowledge of harnessing electricity. To substantiate their claims, they point to certain ancient Egyptian temple artworks, which they interpret as depictions of light bulbs. This theory posits that the Egyptians had invented light bulbs, but this knowledge was later lost. Such conspiracy theories tend to arise when concrete evidence is lacking. In this case, the artwork in question portrays Egyptian mythological stories rather than electrical appliances.

Another theory posits that the pyramids were grain storage facilities. This idea was famously proposed by American politician Ben Carson in 1998, who suggested that the pyramids were constructed by Joseph, the father of Jesus Christ, to store grains. These theories are often the result of political figures seeking to appease religious sentiments. However, the consensus among historians is unequivocal: the primary purpose of the Great Pyramid of Giza was as a tomb.

Now, we arrive at the most enigmatic question: How were these pyramids constructed? The manner in which these structures, rising to 147 meters, with massive stones weighing between 2.5 to 80 tonnes each, were meticulously carved and evenly stacked in the absence of modern tools and the use of wheels is an enigma. Additionally, these feats were accomplished within a mere 20 years. The Great Pyramid of Giza is believed to have been completed in this relatively brief period. Various theories have been put forward to explain this extraordinary achievement. In the following sections, we will explore these theories, excluding the bizarre conspiracy theories, and address the misconceptions portrayed in films depicting the use of slave labor in pyramid construction.

"Poor slaves, subjected to harsh conditions and relentless abuse under the watchful eyes of their supervisors. This image might be familiar from movies and popular narratives. For an extended period in history, it was widely believed that the pyramids were constructed by slaves. Herodotus, a Greek historian from the 5th century BC, was the first to suggest this notion. However, contemporary knowledge has debunked this notion.

In reality, the builders of the pyramids were highly skilled laborers who were well cared for. They received an ample supply of food, which made them stronger and better nourished than the average Egyptian of their time. These laborers resided in nearby communities and received support from various groups, including farmers who assisted with construction during their off-seasons. The people of the kingdom rallied together to support this national project, united in their loyalty to the Pharaoh.

Approximately 20,000 to 30,000 workers toiled for ten hours each day in the construction of the Great Pyramid of Giza.
In terms of construction materials, approximately 5.5 million tonnes of limestone, 8,000 tonnes of granite, and 500,000 tonnes of mortar were employed. These materials were mainly sourced from the surrounding areas, with some brought from Southern Egypt, situated roughly 800 kilometers away.

The process of cutting these rocks was facilitated by the use of copper tools, the prevalent metal of the time. Harder granite stones were fashioned with the assistance of dolerite. Additionally, the builders employed innovative techniques, such as identifying cracks and cavities in the rocks, inserting water-soaked wooden wedges into these fissures, and allowing the expanding wedges to fracture the stones.

An essential question arises: how were these massive stones transported? As the period lacked wheeled carts, a credible theory suggests that rafts were used to ferry the stones from quarries. Upon arrival at the construction site, these stones were positioned using sledges over wet terrain. This method, unveiled in a 2014 study, is inspired by a 4,500-year-old wooden ramp discovered by a team of English and French archaeologists. This advanced understanding of wet sand's properties—when mixed with water at a specific ratio of 2% to 5%—reduces friction between the surface and the objects being pulled.

Another puzzle involves the means of stacking these stones upon one another. The common approach involves using a pulley system, which was effective in theory. However, wheels as we know them today did not exist in Egypt during the 4th Dynasty, apart from pottery wheels. The absence of wheels led to the development of an efficient ramp system. One theory proposes a long, straight slope, accompanied by a system of wooden pillars on either side, allowing ropes to be used for hoisting the stones. This is depicted in ancient artwork from the tomb of Djehutihotep, indicating water being poured onto the sand in front of the sledges, which the physicists Daniel Bonn and his team found to reduce friction, supporting the validity of this theory. Scholars also suggest that each time a new layer of the pyramid was completed, a new slope was fashioned, and its tilt was kept minimal by creating longer slopes.

Furthermore, it is speculated that levers were utilized to stack the stones. The principle involves creating a fulcrum with a high midpoint and a long pole weighted on one end, which facilitated lifting and placing stones. This method is reminiscent of the ancient Egyptian 'shadoof' mechanism used for drawing water from the Nile to irrigate fields.

While these theories seem plausible, they are incomplete in explaining the precise construction methods. Furthermore, the construction timeframe poses a significant challenge to these theories. The Great Pyramid was completed in a mere 20 years. If each stone required transportation using these techniques, a stone had to be placed every 3 minutes, every day, throughout the year, which appears highly improbable.

Ultimately, the construction of the pyramids remains a mystery to this day. Both of these theories seem valid, but they do not fully elucidate the entire process. What is known is that the bottom layers were assembled without the use of mortar, with mortar added to the subsequent layers to enhance structural stability, allowing the pyramids to withstand the test of time, including multiple earthquakes.

A lingering mystery relates to the mortar's composition; while scientists understand the chemistry, they have been unable to replicate it. Finally, the outermost layer of the pyramids was made from fine, white limestone, which reflected sunlight brilliantly, creating a radiant white appearance. This effect has faded over thousands of years, yet some remnants of the white layer remain visible on the Pyramid of Khafre.

Transitioning from the construction aspects, let's delve into the architectural design of the pyramids.

"It's undeniably captivating. Were you aware that the pyramids possess an extraordinary architectural feature? They are meticulously oriented to face precisely North, East, South, and West, with a minuscule margin of error, merely one-fifteenth of a degree. The precision in aligning the pyramids with these cardinal directions is a remarkable achievement, particularly given the absence of compasses and modern technology like GPS during that era.

Researchers have ventured to propose theoretical explanations for this astounding level of precision. One prevailing theory revolves around the use of the Autumn Equinox, a celestial event when Earth's axial tilt results in equal day and night lengths. During the Autumn Equinox, shadows cast on the ground align perfectly with the East and West directions. It is conjectured that the Egyptians could have employed this phenomenon to align the pyramids accurately, with the degree of error in the pyramid's orientation matching the shadows during this astronomical event.

Another theory delves into the realm of constellations. Proponents of this theory suggest that the ancient Egyptians used the stars in the night sky to guide their architectural designs. In 1989, Robert Bauval, an author and Egyptology enthusiast, introduced the Orion Correlation Theory. This theory posits that the three pyramids at Giza were intentionally aligned to mimic the three stars in Orion's Belt. According to this theory, the ancient Egyptians possessed a profound understanding of astronomy, observing and studying celestial bodies, and even coordinating agricultural activities with the positions of stars.

However, it is worth noting that the Orion Correlation Theory is considered a fringe theory, meaning it falls outside the mainstream consensus. Critics argue that the three Giza pyramids were not conceived and built simultaneously, and empirical astronomical observations in 1999 revealed that the pyramids do not align perfectly with the Orion's Belt stars. This discrepancy can be attributed to the gradual shifts in the position of constellations over thousands of years.

This theory serves as a classic example of human attempts to discern patterns even in cases where none exist. When concrete evidence is scarce, and a precise explanation remains elusive, we tend to generate our hypotheses, seeking connections wherever possible, and as a result, we may come to accept these notions as factual. When this inclination is taken to extremes, it leads to peculiar theories, such as the belief that aliens constructed the pyramids, as some contend that the monumental achievement was beyond human capability.

In my view, such theories run counter to the principles of scientific thinking. They represent a shortcut approach to resolving unanswered questions in the absence of compelling evidence. A more prudent approach involves acknowledging the established facts, clearly delineating what remains unknown, and thereby providing a foundation for future generations of archaeologists and historians to conduct thorough research and unveil comprehensive solutions and explanations for these enduring mysteries.

10. One Small Step: The Apollo 11 Moon Landing Enigma

On the 20th of July 1969, a historic event unfolded as the Lunar Module of the Apollo 11 mission made its remarkable landing on the moon's surface. Two intrepid astronauts, Neil Armstrong and Buzz Aldrin, were aboard this spacecraft. Upon successfully landing, Neil Armstrong embarked on a momentous task – opening the lunar module's door to set foot on the moon's surface. This seemingly simple act proved to be quite a challenge due to the high pressure, but after some effort, Armstrong managed to pry the door open.

However, as he attempted to make his way down to the lunar surface, the cramped exit led to an inadvertent mishap. Armstrong's spacesuit collided with the module's top, resulting in a crucial piece of the lunar module breaking off. The astronauts remained oblivious to this development due to the moon's lack of atmosphere, which meant that sounds couldn't travel, rendering them unable to hear the damage caused.

Now, the significance of this broken piece cannot be understated. It happened to be the Ascent Engine Arming Switch. Without this crucial component, the Lunar Module wouldn't be able to return to Earth, leaving Armstrong and Aldrin stranded on the moon.

Undeterred by this mishap, Neil Armstrong proceeded to become the very first human to set foot on the moon, famously declaring, "That's one small step for man, one giant leap for mankind." This iconic moment marked a pivotal achievement in human history.

But here's where things take an intriguing turn. Even today, more than half a century later, there are individuals who refuse to accept that the Apollo 11 mission was a genuine accomplishment. These skeptics contend that it was an elaborate hoax staged by the United States, filmed on Earth, and disseminated as a false narrative to the world.

To bolster their arguments, they point to seemingly baffling anomalies, such as the sight of the American flag appearing to flutter in the airless lunar environment. The question then arises: What is the truth behind these claims? In this Chapter, we endeavor to unravel this fascinating tale.

The genesis of the Apollo 11 mission is closely tied to a larger context – the Cold War, a protracted struggle between the United States and the Soviet Union. This battle extended into the realm of space exploration, with both nations engaged in a fervent Space Race. In 1957, the Soviet Union made a pivotal leap by launching Sputnik, the first artificial satellite, into Earth's orbit. The United States, taken aback by this Soviet accomplishment, swiftly followed suit with its satellite launch in 1958.

In 1961, the Soviets delivered yet another surprise when Cosmonaut Yuri Gagarin became the first human to journey into space. This milestone further reinforced the Soviet Union's lead in the Space Race. In response, U.S. President John F. Kennedy issued a resounding challenge to his nation. In a speech dated 25th May 1961, he pledged to send humans to the moon and return them safely to Earth before the decade's end.

This audacious commitment, made at a time when technology was far less advanced, represented a monumental undertaking. Over the next five years, President Kennedy allocated substantial funds, amounting to $7-$9 billion, to the space program. The entire endeavor was dedicated to realizing this ambitious lunar goal.

The quest began with a series of rigorous tests, commencing with trials of the powerful rockets that would propel astronauts beyond Earth's orbit. Trials of the heat shields for the command modules were conducted to gauge their ability to withstand the intense reentry heat. Propulsion systems for the service module were meticulously examined. Additionally, several unmanned missions, including Apollo 4, Apollo 5, and Apollo 6, were executed for further testing.

Despite a tragic setback when the Apollo 1 mission ended in a cabin fire in January 1967, claiming the lives of three astronauts, NASA continued undeterred. Subsequent missions included the successful Apollo 7 in October 1968, the lunar orbit mission of Apollo 8 in December 1968, and the crucial testing of the lunar module during the Apollo 9 mission in March 1969. Two months later, in May 1969, Apollo 10 rehearsed almost all the actions to be executed during Apollo 11, except for the actual moon landing.

This relentless sequence of missions, with NASA launching a new one every few months, underscored their unwavering commitment to the lunar endeavor. All the meticulous testing and preparation culminated on the 16th of July 1969 when the Apollo 11 mission was launched, bearing three brave astronauts on its historic voyage.

"Commander Neil Armstrong, at 38 years old, was at the helm of this monumental mission, leading the way. Alongside him were two remarkable astronauts: Michael Collins, who piloted the Command Module, and Edwin 'Buzz' Aldrin, the pilot of the Lunar Module. These names are etched into the annals of history, with Neil Armstrong and Buzz Aldrin becoming household names worldwide. However, Michael Collins is not as widely recognized, and the reason behind this is quite intriguing, which I'll reveal later in this chapter.

The Apollo 11 spacecraft was composed of three essential components: the Command Module, the Service Module, and the Lunar Module. The first two were collectively referred to as the Command and Service Module (CSM). The objective was to separate the Lunar Module and enable it to land on the moon. After the lunar mission, the Lunar Module had to be relaunched and reconnected to the CSM for the astronauts' return journey to Earth. To launch this remarkable spacecraft into space, the powerful Saturn V-5 rocket was employed.

Before liftoff, the rocket was loaded with an astonishing 1 million gallons of Kerosene, Liquid Oxygen, and Liquid Hydrogen. The weight of this colossal rocket was an astounding 3 million kilograms. It took less than 10 minutes for this mighty rocket to propel the spacecraft into Earth's orbit. Subsequently, the astronauts completed approximately 1.5 orbits around Earth. After this, the mission control on Earth, responsible for overseeing the mission, gave them the green light to commence the Trans-Lunar Injection – the critical maneuver to propel the spacecraft out of Earth's orbit and toward the moon's orbit. The third stage of the Saturn V-5 rocket was employed to achieve this pivotal step, and all of this unfolded within just five hours of the initial launch.

However, the actual journey to reach the moon took several days, during which the astronauts resided within the spacecraft. They ate, slept, and even documented their experiences and surroundings through photographs. Finally, on the 19th of July 1969, after covering a distance of nearly 400,000 kilometers, the Apollo 11 spacecraft arrived in lunar orbit.

Upon reaching lunar orbit, a momentous event was slated to occur – the separation of the spacecraft into two distinct modules. The Command and Service Module, nicknamed 'Columbia,' retained its position in lunar orbit, with Michael Collins aboard. In contrast, the Lunar Module, affectionately known as 'Eagle,' was designated for landing on the moon, carrying Neil Armstrong and Buzz Aldrin. Importantly, the decision meant that only Armstrong and Aldrin would have the opportunity to set foot on the moon, and not Michael Collins. Perhaps this explains why Michael Collins is not as well-known, despite his pivotal role in the Apollo mission. Despite not stepping on the moon's surface, Collins played arguably the most crucial part of the mission because the Lunar Module needed to rejoin the CSM for the safe return of the astronauts to Earth.

At 8 PM, the Lunar Module was scheduled to commence its descent to the moon. However, at precisely 8:10 PM, alarms began to sound, signaling '1201' and '1202' errors. Neither Armstrong nor Aldrin initially understood the significance of these alarms and promptly contacted mission control for guidance. The response from mission control was to proceed with the mission, reassuring the astronauts by saying, "We're GO." It was later determined that the

'1202' alarm indicated that the guidance computer's processing system was overloaded. Thankfully, the computer had been ingeniously designed to prioritize critical mission programs, ensuring that they would continue functioning despite the overload. Among these critical programs was the automatic landing system, which would facilitate the Lunar Module's touchdown on the lunar surface.

Yet, when the Lunar Module descended to a mere 150 meters above the moon's surface, Neil Armstrong made the momentous decision to assume manual control. He had noticed that the planned landing area was riddled with large boulders, necessitating an immediate change in landing location. The landing site was shifted to an alternative spot situated four miles away from the original target. At 8:16 PM, Buzz Aldrin closely monitored the fuel gauge and discovered that only 5% of the fuel supply remained. The mission control initiated a countdown, ultimately deciding whether to proceed with the landing or abort the mission. Armstrong sent a radio message to Earth with only 30 seconds remaining in this critical countdown, proclaiming, 'Roger, Tranquility.' With a mere 30 seconds left, the Eagle successfully touched down on the lunar surface. This historic moment was broadcast and witnessed by an astounding 650 million people worldwide.

After the landing, Neil Armstrong donned his spacesuit, exited the Lunar Module, and took his monumental first step on the moon. His words, 'That's one small step for man, one giant leap for mankind,' were beamed to an audience of millions. Buzz Aldrin followed suit, and together, they spent the next 2.5 hours conducting experiments, collecting moon dust and rock samples, taking photographs, and setting up scientific instruments.

Although the backdrop of the Cold War was a significant factor in the moon landing, it's important to note that the mission had profound scientific objectives. The astronauts deployed a television camera on the moon to transmit signals to Earth, measured solar winds reaching the moon, initiated laser beams to gauge Earth-moon distance, placed a passive seismometer to monitor moonquakes, and collected a remarkable 23 kilograms of lunar rock and dust. Additionally, they left behind an American flag and a plaque with the inscription, 'Here, Men from the Planet Earth, First set foot upon the Moon. July 1969 A.D.'

The Lunar Module had to remain on the moon for 21 hours before being relaunched and reconnected to the CSM. However, upon returning to the Lunar Module, Armstrong and Aldrin encountered a significant problem – the switch to activate the engine had broken off when they had disembarked. This issue was mentioned at the start of the chapter. Realizing the situation, they promptly informed mission control and began working on a solution.

Their solution was ingenious and relied on understanding the function of a switch. In essence, a switch serves to complete an electrical circuit. Buzz Aldrin noticed that if they could create a connection to reestablish the circuit, the engine could be reignited. Searching for a suitable tool, he spotted his ballpoint pen. They used the pen to restore the connection and successfully reignited the engine.

With the Lunar Module's engine functioning, it was ready to be reconnected to the Command and Service Module. This vital step was necessary for Armstrong, Aldrin, and Collins to return safely to Earth.

The three astronauts initiated the spacecraft's journey back towards Earth. The plan for their Earth re-entry was straightforward: separate the Command Module and the Service Module, and let the Service Module disintegrate in Earth's atmosphere. However, there was a significant concern. If the Service Module suffered severe damage, its debris could pose a collision risk to the Command Module, potentially resulting in the death of the astronauts onboard. To mitigate this risk, NASA equipped the Service Module with thrusters to propel it far away from the Command Module, ensuring that they wouldn't collide.

But as the astronauts began their return to Earth, they discovered that the thrusters on the Service Module were malfunctioning.

Consequently, they had to remain in the Command Module while witnessing the Service Module breaking apart and its debris floating perilously close. It was a miraculous turn of events that none of the debris collided with the Command Module, ensuring the astronauts' safety. The perilous nature of the mission was such that then-U.S. President Nixon had a contingency speech prepared in case the astronauts didn't survive. This alternate speech contemplated the possibility that Neil Armstrong and Edwin Aldrin wouldn't return from the moon. Fortunately, this speech was never needed, as the Command Module successfully re-entered Earth's atmosphere. Parachutes were deployed, and the Command Module safely landed in the ocean. All three astronauts were alive and unharmed, with rescue ships evacuating them from the ocean. Their return was truly a remarkable achievement, considering the numerous challenges they faced throughout the mission.

After their return, the three astronauts were placed in quarantine for two weeks, during which they were not allowed contact with other humans due to concerns about potential pathogens, viruses, or bacteria they might have encountered on the moon. Fortunately, there were no health complications resulting from this quarantine.

Apollo 11's successful moon landing became headline news in newspapers around the world. U.S. President Kennedy's promise to have humans reach the moon before the end of the decade had been realized, thanks to NASA's remarkable efforts.

Although some conspiracy theories have suggested that the moon landing was a hoax, these claims have been thoroughly debunked. Notably, the Soviet Union, a major competitor in the space race, acknowledged the moon landing's authenticity in the Great Soviet Encyclopedia. The encyclopedia, published between 1970 and 1979, referenced the moon landing multiple times as a factual event. In fact, Soviet articles recognized the Apollo landing as the third historic event of the space age, following the launch of Sputnik in 1957 and Yuri Gagarin's flight in 1961.

Some conspiracy theories have focused on specific aspects of the moon landing, such as the appearance of the American flag, the lack of stars in photos, the perceived inconsistencies in shadow angles, and questions about the cameras used. However, these issues have logical explanations. The appearance of the flag on the moon is attributed to the design of a horizontal rod to keep it extended, and its apparent fluttering is due to the flag's unique design and movement caused by the astronauts. The absence of stars in photos is explained by the fact that the moon landing occurred during daylight hours when sunlight illuminated the lunar surface and the astronauts' reflective spacesuits. The perceived shadow inconsistencies are attributed to the scattering of light from both the Sun and the moon's surface, as well as the limitations of the cameras used.

It's important to distinguish between unfounded conspiracy theories and legitimate criticisms. While the moon landing faced its share of criticism, it was a monumental achievement, and the scientific and historical consensus supports its authenticity.

In January 1962, the New York Times published an article that brought into question the vast sums of money allocated for the moon mission. The article pointed out that the resources being invested in lunar exploration could have been used to establish approximately 120 universities the size of Harvard. It posed a critical inquiry: Should such a significant financial commitment be made to reach the moon, or would it be more prudent to establish Harvard-sized universities in every state in the United States? The central criticism revolved around whether this massive financial allocation was justified when the nation faced numerous pressing issues, such as education, income inequality, and the repercussions of the Vietnam War.

Yet, unbeknownst to many at the time, the moon landing held hidden benefits that extended far beyond the lunar surface. One such benefit was the advancement of computer chip technology. In the early 1960s, three years after the invention of microchips, IBM had decided against incorporating them into their computers. However, NASA's substantial orders for integrated circuits prompted IBM to reconsider, which subsequently led to a more than 90% price reduction over the following five years. The rigorous testing of computer chips for the Apollo program demonstrated their reliability for critical functions, laying the foundation for their widespread use in various applications.

The technological leaps resulting from the moon landing were exponential. It proved that computers, relying on integrated circuits, could safely transport astronauts to the moon and back, reinforcing confidence in this technology for everyday life.

Nonetheless, only three years after the historic Apollo 11 mission, in December 1972, Apollo 17 marked the final moon mission. In the nearly 50 years since then, no human has returned to the lunar surface. This prolonged absence serves as a testament to the immense expense of the Apollo program. With more than 400,000 engineers, scientists, and technicians involved, the total cost at the time was $24 billion, equivalent to over $100 billion in today's currency.

Initially, criticism was primarily confined to journalists, but as the average person's fascination with NASA and the moon waned, it became evident that a reallocation of funds was required. This shift in public sentiment was in part due to the continuing Vietnam War and the rising challenges faced by the American populace. The expense of space programs was increasingly perceived as a misallocation of resources, and political leaders were compelled to listen to the concerns of their constituents.

In December 2017, former President Donald Trump initially voiced a plan to increase funding for a lunar return mission by 2024. However, he later modified this stance, advocating for NASA to prioritize a Mars mission. Nevertheless, after almost five decades, NASA has revitalized its commitment to lunar exploration with the Artemis program. They plan to begin with unmanned rocket testing and have set a goal to send the first woman to the moon by 2025-2026. Subsequently, they aim to send the first person of color to the lunar surface as well.

One thing remains certain: the return of humans to the moon is anticipated before the decade's end, rekindling our exploration of Earth's celestial neighbor.

11. Supersonic Broke: The Concorde Plane Crash

On the fateful day of July 25, 2000, around 4 PM, Air France flight 4590 was poised for takeoff. This flight was not your ordinary passenger journey; it was the domain of the Supersonic Concorde, an aircraft capable of traversing the skies at twice the speed of sound. To put this into perspective, it streaked through the air like a bullet fired from a gun. Whereas typical passenger flights on conventional planes took a leisurely 8 hours to make the voyage from Paris to New York, the Supersonic Concorde slashed that time to a mere 3.5 hours. But there was an unmistakable distinction about this flight—it was an opulent experience, reserved for the affluent. Traveling on the Concorde was the epitome of luxury, far beyond the reach of the average person, as a round-trip ticket between Paris and New York would set you back $12,000, and this was 22 years ago. Considering inflation, that price tag would equate to roughly $20,000 in today's currency. This ticket amounted to over ₹1.5 million, and as the clock ticked to 4:40 PM, the aircraft was ready to embark on its journey.

As the plane began its acceleration along the runway, an unsettling discovery was made by the Air Traffic Controller—a fire had ignited beneath the aircraft. An alert was promptly relayed to the pilot, but it was a case of too little, too late. The plane was already hurtling down the runway at a considerable speed, rendering an abortive takeoff impossible. The pilot, with the grim realization that there was no turning back, radioed the controller to convey that the plane could not be stopped. In mere seconds, the aircraft soared into the sky, the fire escalating to an uncontrollable blaze. The pilots made desperate attempts to regain control, disengaging certain engines, but the aircraft was unable to achieve the required velocity. Onlookers on the highway adjacent to the airport witnessed the horrifying spectacle unfolding before their eyes. In a matter of minutes, the situation deteriorated to a point where the pilots lost all command over the aircraft. Tragically, the Concorde crashed into a hotel located 15 kilometers from Paris. This harrowing accident claimed the lives of all 100 passengers aboard, as well as the lives of the 9 crew members.

The devastating outcome of the crash reverberated around the globe, as the world grappled with the loss.

"The world's most prestigious aircraft crashes. More than 100 people are dead." The Concorde crash sent shockwaves throughout the world, leaving people incredulous. How could this happen? The Concorde was the epitome of aviation prestige—the crème de la crème of aircraft, renowned for its Supersonic capabilities. However, the crash of this one aircraft irrevocably transformed the trajectory of Supersonic aviation.

Breaking the Sound Barrier
My friends, the term 'supersonic' is inextricably linked with sound, specifically the speed of sound. Ordinarily, the speed of sound at sea level hovers at approximately 1,236 kilometers per hour, with some minor fluctuations depending on air temperature. The classification of aircraft speed falls into four broad categories: Subsonic for speeds lower than the speed of sound, Transonic for speeds around the speed of sound, Supersonic for speeds exceeding the speed of sound, and Hypersonic for speeds surpassing five times the speed of sound. It is important to note that the unit of measure for this speed is known as the Mach number, which signifies the ratio between an aircraft's speed and the speed of sound.

The typical passenger aircraft in which we embark travel at speeds of approximately 900 kilometers per hour, classifying them as Subsonic. The Concorde, which I reference in the past tense since it is no longer in operation (and I shall delve into the reasons later in this narrative), boasted speeds of around 2,160 kilometers per hour, placing it in the Supersonic realm with a Mach number close to 2.0. For a captivating tidbit of information, the current title-holder for the world's fastest aircraft is the Lockheed SR 71 Blackbird, with a staggering Mach number of 3.3, equating to over 3,500 kilometers per hour. The SR 71 Blackbird stands as a model for Supersonic speed. Furthermore, an exciting development is the SR 72, the next generation of this aircraft, currently in the developmental phase. It is projected to embark on its inaugural test flight in 2025, with an anticipated speed exceeding Mach 6.0, which amounts to approximately 7,400 kilometers per hour. Consequently, the SR 72 will be classified in the Hypersonic category, considering speeds ranging from Mach 5.0 to Mach 10.0.

The Sonic Boom

A most intriguing facet of Supersonic aircraft is the phenomenon of the sonic boom. When these aircraft breach the sound barrier, they generate a sonic boom, an auditory event that leaves an indelible impression. This signature boom occurs due to the aircraft's ability to outpace sound waves. As a passenger jet moves through the air at Subsonic speeds, sound waves assume a particular curvature. However, when an aircraft is capable of Supersonic velocities, the intensity of its speed leads to the overlapping of sound waves. This collision of sound waves produces an abrupt, deafening noise akin to a thunderous explosion, heralding the passage of a Supersonic aircraft. For individuals on the ground underneath the path of a Supersonic jet, the experience is unmistakable—listening to the sonic boom is akin to hearing an enormous sonic clap, reminiscent of a balloon bursting as air pressure is suddenly released.

The visual accompaniment often associated with Supersonic travel is the formation of vapor clouds surrounding the aircraft during flight. Nevertheless, these cloud formations can also be a feature of Transonic aircraft under specific conditions. This effect occurs when Transonic planes traverse moist air. In situations of elevated humidity, the plummeting air pressure around the wings is accompanied by a corresponding temperature drop. This atmospheric interplay prompts moisture in the air to coalesce into visible cloud formations. Although these cloud formations can indeed occur in proximity to Supersonic aircraft breaking the sound barrier, it is imperative to comprehend that the mere presence of these cloud formations does not signify Supersonic flight.

I will now proceed to expound on the turn of events following the Concorde crash and its enduring implications.

History of Supersonic Flights

The journey through the annals of Supersonic flights unveils a captivating narrative. While the technology may appear cutting-edge, its origins date back to 1947 when Major Charles Yeager of the US Air Force achieved the remarkable feat of breaking the sound barrier. On October 14th, 1947, he piloted an aircraft at supersonic speeds, heralding a historic moment in aviation history above the Mojave Desert in America.

Following this breakthrough, the world of business magnates and commercial airlines cast a keen eye on supersonic aircraft. Their inquiry was straightforward: Why reserve these marvels of engineering solely for military applications? They aspired to develop supersonic aircraft accessible to ordinary passengers and embarked on a decade-long journey to transform this aspiration into reality.

However, the early 1960s marked a pivotal juncture in this trajectory. The intense Cold War rivalry between the United States and the Soviet Union diverted the focus of the US aerospace industry toward the realm of space exploration. The allure of moon landings and spacecraft eclipsed the quest for supersonic passenger planes, prompting a notable shift in the center of gravity for supersonic developments to Europe.

The Ascent of the Concorde Airliner
A significant turning point occurred when France and Britain joined forces in a multi-billion-dollar agreement for supersonic research. This collaboration materialized with the formal signing of the Concorde Agreement in 1962, a groundbreaking accord. Their collective mission was to construct a supersonic jetliner expressly designed for passenger travel, not military applications.

This vision bore fruit in March 1969 when the Concorde aircraft successfully completed its inaugural flight. Subsequently, over the course of a few years, the Concorde earned the distinction of being the world's premier supersonic passenger flight. It marked a departure from the exclusive domain of the military, opening the skies to civilians who could now experience the thrill of supersonic travel. Underpinned by the slogan "Arrive Before You Leave," the Concorde efficiently bridged the Atlantic Ocean, shuttling passengers between Europe and America in half the time of conventional aircraft.

What set the Concorde apart was its distinctive nose, which could be adjusted by tilting it upwards and downwards. During takeoffs and landings, this dynamic feature ensured optimal visibility for the pilots. When airborne, the nose could be raised to enhance aerodynamics. In terms of capacity, the Concorde was relatively compact, accommodating a mere 100 passengers initially. However, with time, the interior underwent a transformation, evolving from simplicity to luxury. Given the premium cost of tickets, as only the affluent could afford them, the airlines saw fit to enhance the interiors, introducing opulent features like caviar and champagne. Traveling on the Concorde became emblematic of prestige and status, attracting an array of luminaries, including superstars, celebrities, sports icons, and politicians. Notably, even former British Prime Minister Tony Blair embarked on this remarkable aircraft.

During its illustrious career, the Concorde maintained an impeccable safety record, free from any flight incidents for over 25 years. Safety and luxury were twin priorities. However, all of this changed tragically on July 25, 2000, when Air France flight 4590, as previously described, ended in disaster. The plane crashed near Paris, resulting in the loss of all 109 lives on board. Subsequent investigations revealed that a 17-inch metal piece left on the runway by a previous flight had been propelled into the Concorde's tire upon takeoff, initiating a catastrophic sequence of events that led to the crash.

This catastrophic incident sent shockwaves worldwide, as it shattered the widely held belief that flying on the Concorde was inherently safe, akin to the misconception surrounding the "unsinkable" Titanic. Subsequently, both Air France and British Airways chose to temporarily suspend all Concorde flights while investigations unfolded. In November 2001, they cautiously reintroduced Concorde flights, but the industry faced several insurmountable challenges. The crash had cast a pall over the Concorde's reputation, and the September 2001 attacks on the World Trade Center ushered in a period of anxiety and reduced air travel. The Concorde's thunderous sonic boom, a marvel to behold initially, transformed into a source of disturbance for those residing in its flight path. This prompted a shift in flight routes to limit disruptions, directing Concorde flights primarily over the ocean instead of populated land areas.

As a result of these factors, the once-glorious Concorde faced a decline, leading to its eventual downfall.

Fuel consumption posed yet another significant issue for the Concorde. Compared to conventional passenger airplanes, the Concorde's fuel consumption was a staggering four times higher. This was detrimental both from an environmental and economic perspective. To compound these challenges, the costs associated with maintaining and operating these supersonic planes were exorbitant. For instance, British Airways incurred an annual expense of £1 billion back then, which, when adjusted for inflation, amounts to approximately £1.7 billion today.

From a passenger's viewpoint, spending a substantial sum, around ₹1.5 million, for the sake of swift travel seemed less justifiable when confronted with the Concorde's relatively cramped seating. The spacious comfort of business or first-class seats seemed a more appealing option. The Concorde's demand dwindled, further exacerbated by the crash, ultimately leading to increasingly vacant flights.

These myriad challenges culminated in Air France and British Airways jointly deciding to discontinue their Concorde flights in 2003. On October 24, 2003, the last commercial Concorde flight took off, marking the end of an era and signaling the conclusion of supersonic commercial flight.

Strikingly, nearly two decades later, supersonic aircraft are poised for a resurgence. Startups like Boom are actively developing supersonic planes, with United Airlines having placed orders for 15 of Boom's Overture Aircraft, designed to reach Mach 1.7. If these endeavors succeed, supersonic aircraft may return to the skies by 2029. The environmental impact, a pressing concern, is being addressed through the use of sustainable aviation fuels and carbon-neutral manufacturing methods. While the Overture Aircraft may not match the Concorde's Mach 2.0 speed, it will still significantly reduce travel times, potentially shrinking a Dubai-to-Singapore flight from 7 hours to just 4.

In an aviation landscape that often sees technological progress, the revival of supersonic flight demonstrates a unique and promising reversal.

12. Exploring Alien Worlds: James Webb Telescope's Discoveries

Recently, NASA made the captivating and groundbreaking images captured by the James Webb Telescope available to the public. These extraordinary photos offer unique insights into the universe, including the oldest glimpse of our cosmos, reaching back an astonishing 13.1 billion years. Another image has unveiled an alien exoplanet where the presence of water, H_2O, has been detected. In this chapter, let's delve into these remarkable discoveries.

The James Webb Space Telescope stands as the largest and most potent space science telescope ever constructed. Every image it captures represents a new revelation, granting humanity an unparalleled view of the cosmos. With its ability to observe the formation of the universe's first stars and galaxies, the Webb has sparked tremendous excitement and amazement among scientists and enthusiasts alike.

Now, let's delve into the intriguing details of this telescope. The James Webb Space Telescope, with a cost of approximately $10 billion, underwent 25 years of meticulous design and development. Remarkably, it operates under frigid conditions, with a current temperature of -266.75°C, a mere few degrees warmer than the absolute zero temperature limit of -273°C. To maintain this extreme cold, the telescope orbits the Sun rather than the Earth, specifically at the L2 Point, positioned about 1.5 million kilometers from our planet. This location remains in the Earth's shadow, ensuring the necessary temperature conditions. Additionally, an expansive sun shield, nearly the size of a tennis court, blocks out excess sunlight.

One of the most remarkable features of this telescope is its extraordinary focal length, measuring 131.4 meters—more than 2,500 times the focal length of a typical DSLR camera lens. The telescope's main mirror weighs about 705 kg.

The James Webb Space Telescope mainly operates within the infrared portion of the electromagnetic spectrum, encompassing wavelengths from 0.6 to 28 micrometers. This extended wavelength range offers a unique advantage: it enables the telescope to peer through gases and clouds, making it particularly adept at astronomical observations.

The telescope is equipped with two infrared cameras: the Near Infrared Camera (NIRCAM) for capturing shorter infrared wavelengths and the Mid Infrared Instrument (MIRI Cam) for longer wavelengths. These two cameras yield different images due to the variation in wavelengths they capture.

The image captured by NIRCAM is awe-inspiring and garnered substantial attention when initially released. It allows us to witness the death of a star in exquisite detail. In this image, two stars are orbiting each other, with the brighter star in the earlier stages of its life and the dimmer star nearing the end of its life cycle. The dying star has released clouds of gases and dust over thousands of years, forming a structure known as a Planetary Nebula. Due to the gravitational interplay between the stars, this nebula takes on its distinctive shape.

The image captured by MIRI Cam provides a complementary perspective. It reveals the two stars more distinctly while lessening the prominence of the cloud. This effect is due to the longer wavelength of MIRI Cam, enabling it to penetrate the cloud's dense center.

Stars, like humans, undergo a life cycle that progresses through stages such as childhood, adolescence, adulthood, old age, and ultimately, death. Our Sun, which is a star, is currently in its youthful phase, but in about 5 billion years, it will transition into a Red Giant, following a similar path to the stars depicted in the image.

As a Red Giant, our Sun will grow in size and consume the inner planets of Mercury and Venus. Earth's environment will become inhospitable. Ultimately, it will become a planetary nebula, followed by a White Dwarf, and reach the conclusion of its celestial journey.

These astonishing discoveries underscore the tremendous capabilities and scientific potential of the James Webb Space Telescope, offering us unparalleled views of the cosmos and the enigmatic life cycles of stars.

Humans have a generous timespan of 5 billion years to uncover a technology capable of modifying Earth's orbit. But that's a concern for a future era; let's concentrate on the remaining astronomical revelations. NASA recently unveiled a series of captivating images from the James Webb Space Telescope, starting with what is perhaps the most historically significant photograph. This image takes us on a visual journey through 13 billion years of cosmic history.

American President Joe Biden described it as a "new window into the history of the universe." The photograph captures a galaxy cluster known as SMACS 0723. The galaxies closer to our vantage point possess substantial gravitational forces that bend and distort the light behind them, creating an effect called Gravitational Lensing. This phenomenon enables us to observe objects concealed behind the galaxy cluster. However, it wasn't a simple point-and-click process; it took the telescope 12.5 hours to capture this image. It involved taking multiple images at various wavelengths and then combining them into the remarkable composite photo we see.

In this composite image, galaxies appear redder in color the farther they are from us, with redness indicating increased distance. Another notable photograph features Stephan's Quintet, which is a collection of five galaxies, even though the prefix "quin" typically signifies five, it seems more appropriate to call it a Quadtet. This is because the leftmost galaxy in the image lies 40 million light-years away, while the other four galaxies are positioned about 290 million light-years away. The leftmost galaxy appears more vivid and detailed, while the other four galaxies appear somewhat blurred. These four galaxies' proximity to one another has led to their interstellar dust and stars interacting and being affected by each other's gravitational forces. This interaction provides scientists with an intriguing opportunity to study the outcomes when galaxies come into such close proximity.

Perhaps the most exquisite image reveals the birth of a star. Dubbed the "Cosmic Cliffs" by scientists, this image captures the Carina Nebula, a bright area formed by clouds of dust and gases, often likened to a shining cloud or "Niharika" in Hindi. Referring to the life cycle of a star, this image allows us to witness the birth of stars, with the red dots signifying nascent stars. Both the Near Infrared Camera (NIRCAM) and the Mid Infrared Instrument (MIRI Cam) captured this spectacular view.

The most intriguing data, rather than an image, pertains to the exoplanet WASP-96b, located 1,150 light-years away from Earth. Exoplanets are planets outside our solar system. In addition to the two cameras, the James Webb Telescope boasts a Near Infra-Red Imager and Slitless Spectrograph (NIRISS). The NIRISS measured the light emanating from WASP-96b for 6.5 hours, producing a light curve as a result. Analyzing this curve's data revealed the presence of water (H_2O) on the exoplanet, as well as indications of haze and clouds. The ability to determine water's presence on a planet without visual confirmation is grounded in the distinctive wavelengths of light. Each color has a specific wavelength, and the colors we perceive are a product of these wavelengths. Using spectrographs to measure light intensities at these wavelengths provides valuable information. In this instance, the pattern of blocked wavelengths indicated the presence of H_2O on WASP-96b.

However, the outlook for extraterrestrial life on WASP-96b is far from optimistic. The exoplanet's extreme proximity to its star, combined with its size, results in searing temperatures exceeding 530°C. The chances of discovering alien life there are exceedingly remote.

In the coming months, the James Webb Space Telescope will be directed toward a different planet, with the aim of capturing images of what is considered one of the most potentially habitable planets. Theoretical calculations suggest that within our Milky Way galaxy, there could be approximately 300 million potentially habitable planets, where conditions might support human existence and sustain life. However, practical observations have been made on only around 5,000 exoplanets within the Milky Way, and this figure encompasses all observed exoplanets, not just the potentially habitable ones.

Remarkably, in November 2018, researchers identified a specific exoplanet as having the highest probability of being habitable when compared to others. This planet bears the name TRAPPIST-1e and bears the closest resemblance to Earth, making it a compelling candidate for habitability. Located a relatively modest 40 light-years away from Earth, which equates to a staggering 380 trillion kilometers, TRAPPIST-1e is considered within a reasonable distance relative to other exoplanets.

Notably, TRAPPIST-1e orbits an ultra-cool dwarf star known as TRAPPIST-1, which is distinctly cooler than our Sun, hence the "ultra-cool" designation. The separation between the star and the planet is less than Earth's distance from the Sun. Significantly, the planet's temperature falls within the habitable zone, making it conducive to the presence of liquid water. Furthermore, the physical attributes of TRAPPIST-1e closely resemble Earth's, with a radius of 91% and total mass of 77% compared to Earth. The density is approximately 102% of Earth's, and surface gravity measures at 93% of Earth's gravity. The planet is confirmed to have a solid rock surface.

The relatively cold yet not freezing temperatures on this planet allow for the existence of liquid water. In the months ahead, the James Webb Space Telescope will conduct a comprehensive analysis of TRAPPIST-1e. This analysis will focus on examining the planet's atmosphere to detect the presence of specific gases like carbon dioxide, methane, and water vapor. The identification of a particular combination of these gases could suggest the potential for life on this distant planet.

We eagerly anticipate the forthcoming discoveries facilitated by this advanced telescope. Scientists have long believed that to support life, a celestial body should possess three key elements: liquid water, a solid surface, and an atmosphere harboring the right combination of gases. As we await the results, it is clear that exploring such potentially habitable exoplanets holds great promise.

13. Kohinoor's Curse: The World's Most Famous Diamond Mystery

Back in 1854, during the British Colonial rule of India, the then Governor General, Lord Dalhousie, made a rather extraordinary decision. He sent a 15-year-old child from Punjab to England, Prince Duleep Singh, also known as Maharaja Duleep Singh. Lord Dalhousie believed that the child's mother posed a threat and had an unsavory character, which led to the decision to separate him from his mother.

In England, this young prince underwent a significant transformation as he embraced Christianity and forged a close friendship with Queen Victoria's son, Edward VII. The British Crown assumed responsibility for him, providing an annual stipend of £50,000. To put this into perspective with today's inflation, it equates to a remarkable ₹650 million per year.

Prince Duleep Singh was no ordinary boy; he was the last ruler of the Sikh Empire in India. Notably, four years before he was sent to England, in 1849, the British demanded that the 11-year-old Duleep surrender a diamond to Queen Victoria, which happened to be the renowned Kohinoor Diamond. This magnificent gem traveled 6,700 kilometers on a ship from India to London, marking the beginning of its infamous history.

Legend has it that the Kohinoor Diamond comes with a curious superstition known as the "Curse of Koh-i-noor." The belief is that "he who owns this diamond will own the world, but will also know all its misfortunes." Throughout its history, the diamond has been associated with bloodshed, violence, and betrayals, making it one of the most infamous diamonds in history.

Now, we will delve into the intriguing story of the Kohinoor Diamond, tracing its journey from India to England, where it now resides in the Tower of London's Jewel House. Over the years, there have been numerous demands to return the Kohinoor Diamond to India, but it remains a contentious issue.

There are several theories regarding the diamond's origin. While some believe it dates back to the time of Lord Krishna, historians generally accept that it was discovered in the Kollur Mines, situated in the Golconda region. Golconda was renowned for its diamond mines, and during the 18th century, it was the world's sole source for diamonds, until similar mines were found in Brazil in 1725.

However, the exact discovery date of the Kohinoor remains elusive, with historians estimating its origins between 1100-1300. The first documented mention of the diamond was in a Hindu text in 1306, though the text's name and author remain unknown. In 1526, the first Mughal emperor, Babur, mentioned the diamond in his Baburnama, referring to it as worth half the daily expenses of the entire world. Shah Jahan, in 1628, commissioned the iconic Peacock Throne, on which the Kohinoor and the Timur Ruby were prominently featured.

It wasn't until 1739, when Nadir Shah of Persia invaded Delhi, that the diamond became part of his loot. Nadir Shah carried away an immense treasure, including the Kohinoor, which he had learned of through an insider's tip that it was hidden in Mohammed Shah's turban. The diamond fell to the ground during a proposed turban exchange, dazzling Nadir Shah with its brilliance and leading him to utter "Koh-i-Nur," meaning Mountain of Light. This is how the diamond acquired its name.

Over the next 70 years, the Kohinoor resided in present-day Afghanistan. The diamond's grim reputation, known as the Curse of Kohinoor, began to emerge. The belief was that the diamond brought immense power to its owner, yet misfortune would inevitably follow.

While the origin story of the name may be in doubt, it is factual that Nadir Shah bestowed the name Kohinoor upon the diamond. The diamond's history continued to be turbulent and took various twists and turns.

The journey of the Kohinoor Diamond is steeped in historical intrigue, and its legacy continues to be a subject of debate. Whether it will ever return to its place of origin in India remains a matter of conjecture and negotiation.

As you'll soon discover, there is some truth to this tale. Misfortune did indeed cast its shadow upon Nadir Shah in 1747 when he was killed by his own guard, leading to the collapse of his empire. Ahmad Shah Durrani, also known as Ahmad Khan Abdali, a member of Nadir Shah's army, emerged as the founder of a new Afghan empire, along with being the new possessor of the Kohinoor diamond.

Intriguingly, the curse of Kohinoor or perhaps other factors, led to disputes even within the Durrani empire. While Ahmad's son, Timur, effectively managed the empire, later generations were embroiled in conflicts for the throne. Zaman Shah Durrani, Timur's son and the third ruler, was subjected to the cruel fate of being blinded with hot needles. Subsequently, Shuja Shah Durrani, the fifth ruler and brother of Zaman Shah, found himself in possession of the Kohinoor.

Shuja Shah Durrani's wife famously commented on the Kohinoor's unparalleled value. She likened it to a scenario where a strong man could cast four pebbles in four directions (North, South, East, and West), then toss a fifth pebble into the air. If the space enclosed by these five pebbles were to be filled with gold, the gold's value would still not match that of the Kohinoor.

In 1809, Shuja Shah Durrani was dethroned and sought refuge in Lahore under Maharaja Ranjit Singh, the founder of the Sikh Empire. In exchange for this refuge, Ranjit Singh requested the Kohinoor diamond, and so it became a part of the Sikh empire in 1813.

Kohinoor held significant symbolic value for Ranjit Singh, who had reclaimed the lands previously controlled by the Durrani dynasty. Known as the Lion of Lahore or Sher-e-Punjab, Ranjit Singh wore the Kohinoor on his bicep in an armlet.

In the early 19th century, the grip of the East India Company over India was strengthening. Upon learning of Ranjit Singh's death in 1839 and his intention to gift the diamond to Hindu priests, the British were deeply concerned. British newspapers of the time were indignant, with one publication describing the diamond as "the richest, most costly gem in the known world, [entrusted] to the trust of a profane, idolatrous, and mercenary priesthood."

Consequently, the British government directed the East India Company to monitor the whereabouts of the Kohinoor diamond, with the aim of acquiring it for the British treasury.

The British had to be patient, as it took nearly a decade for the opportunity to arise. By 1843, the only contenders for the Punjabi throne were Rani Jindan, Ranjit Singh's wife, and a five-year-old child, Prince Duleep Singh. Following the conclusion of the second Anglo-Sikh war in 1849, the East India Company put an end to the rule of the Punjab empire.

At the time, Duleep Singh was around ten years old and was made to sign a Treaty of Lahore. According to this treaty, the Kohinoor diamond was to be surrendered to the East India Company. Punjab was the last major state to fall under British control, and after their victory, the British were determined to prevent any resurgence of the Sikh Empire. They imprisoned Jindan and sent Duleep Singh to London, where he was converted to Christianity.

As I mentioned earlier in the chapter, when Duleep Singh was a mere 15 years old, he was transported to London in 1854. During his stay, while his portrait was being painted at Buckingham Palace in July 1854, Queen Victoria allowed him to see the Kohinoor once again. Holding it in his hands, it is said that Duleep Singh uttered the words,

In the later years of his life, Duleep Singh rebelled against the British and sought to return to India, even trying to secure help from the Germans, but his efforts proved fruitless. He passed away under unfortunate circumstances at the age of 55 in Paris, living in poverty.

In contrast, the Kohinoor became a cherished possession of Queen Victoria. Interestingly, the legend surrounding the "curse of Kohinoor" suggested that only a God or a woman could wear it without facing adverse consequences. Consequently, when the British monarchy was passed to a male, the Queen Consort would wear the Kohinoor.

Over the years, with the change of monarchs, the Kohinoor always passed to the reigning Queen, eventually becoming part of the Crown Jewels. It initially adorned Queen Alexandra's crown, followed by Queen Mary's. In 1937, it was integrated into the crown worn by the mother of the present Queen of England.

The last public sighting of this crown, with the Kohinoor, was during the Queen Mother's funeral in 2002. Currently, you can find this crown, along with the Kohinoor, in the Waterloo barracks at the Tower of London.

Located within the Jewel House, the Kohinoor has been safeguarded for the past 800 years. Among all the owners throughout its history, the British monarchy holds the distinction of possessing the Kohinoor for a record 173 years.

For many Indians, the Kohinoor diamond carries deep emotional significance. Shashi Tharoor's memorable 2015 speech at the Oxford Union resonated widely, emphasizing the stark economic decline experienced by India during British colonial rule. He highlighted the economic prowess that India represented when the British first arrived, accounting for 23% of the world economy. However, by the time the British departed, India's share had dwindled to less than 4%. India had become a primary source of British economic gains, serving as the largest buyer of British goods and exports.

Prime Minister Modi also commended Tharoor's arguments, shedding light on the economic and prosperity opportunities lost due to British colonialism. Today, the Kohinoor symbolizes this era of British colonial rule. The debate arises from whether the British acquired the Kohinoor through theft from India or as part of a mutually agreed deal.

A year following Shashi Tharoor's 2015 speech, in 2016, an NGO filed a petition in the Supreme Court, urging the Indian government to seek the return of the Kohinoor from the British government. However, Ranjith Kumar, the government's representative, argued that the diamond was acquired through the Lahore Treaty, neither stolen nor forcefully taken, making any efforts to retrieve it futile. Subsequently, the Archaeological Survey of India, on behalf of the government, expressed its intent to pursue the return of the Kohinoor through diplomatic channels, distancing itself from Mr. Kumar's stance.

From a legal perspective, there are no clear grounds for the Kohinoor's return to India, as the only legal avenue involves the 1970 UNESCO Convention. This convention primarily pertains to cultural property illicitly transported after 1970 and is not retrospective. Moreover, it is unclear which country should be the rightful recipient, given the complex historical border changes and the fact that present-day India, Afghanistan, and Pakistan only emerged as sovereign territories post-independence.

Kohinoor's fate raises questions about which country it should be returned to. The Taliban in Afghanistan expressed their desire to have it back in 2000. In 2016, a petition was lodged in Pakistan's Lahore High Court, claiming that the British had taken the Kohinoor from what is now Pakistan, as the capital of the Sikh empire was in Lahore. Anthropologist Richard Kurin suggests that, logically, several countries, including Afghanistan, Pakistan, India, and even Iran, have valid claims to the diamond. Still, these modern-day nations did not exist at the time of its removal, even though the regions did.

Kurin emphasizes that from both a historical and emotional perspective, it may be best to let go of the Kohinoor permanently. Doing so would serve as a symbolic gesture to prevent the repetition of its dark history and allow it to rest peacefully in its final resting place.

14. Ghosts Unveiled: The Science Behind the Paranormal

In 1989, iconic Hollywood stars like Harrison Ford, Julia Roberts, and Robert De Niro were engaged in the production of a cinematic masterpiece. This film, titled "Ethereal Enigma," fell within the realm of drama and mystery, revolving around the concept of spirits trapped in an ancient mansion, yearning for salvation. The enchanting backdrop for this project was a majestic palace located in Jaipur, India.

On one seemingly ordinary evening, after the day's filming had concluded, and the sun had gracefully surrendered to the night, Julia Roberts sought solace in her cozy trailer. It was during this tranquil moment that she experienced something truly extraordinary. She claims to have observed a woman seated at the edge of her bed, engaging in a surreal conversation. The eerie aura surrounding this presence led Julia to believe she was in the company of a ghostly apparition.

This tale is but a single thread in a vast tapestry of countless anecdotes from around the world. People from diverse walks of life assert that they have encountered ghosts and spirits, even engaging in dialogues with these ethereal beings. Such paranormal experiences have been reported by many, with their stories often serving as inspiration for a myriad of films. Cinematic titles like "The Sixth Sense," "The Shining," and "Poltergeist" often proudly claim to be "inspired by real events." Television shows like "Ghosthunters" follow individuals armed with cutting-edge equipment on quests to apprehend otherworldly entities, employing technology to substantiate the existence of these entities. Additionally, various individuals have taken to YouTube, sharing videos of their conversations with departed souls, as demonstrated by prominent American paranormal expert Sarah Thompson, who maintains that she has communicated with the spirit of the late Hollywood legend, James Stewart.

Now, the critical question emerges: What is the actual truth underlying these enigmatic encounters? In this presentation, we endeavor to embark on a journey towards comprehension.

Firstly, it is imperative to set aside instances where events possess clear, rational explanations. An exemplar of this is the well-documented case of the Fox Sisters. In the 1800s, in the United States, three sisters, renowned as the Fox Sisters, gained widespread recognition within the spiritual community. These sisters were believed to possess the extraordinary ability to communicate with ghosts and spirits from a tender age. They became sought-after mediums for those seeking contact with the deceased. During their sessions, peculiar phenomena were observed, such as unexplained rapping sounds on the walls and the appearance of messages on blank cards. Their spirit communication sessions captivated the American public and generated substantial income. However, a turning point occurred when one of the sisters' husbands, an orthodox Christian, passed away, expressing his disapproval of their spiritual activities. Subsequently, one of the sisters spiraled into depression, alcoholism, and estrangement from her siblings. Eventually, she confessed publicly that the three sisters had been perpetuating a prolonged hoax. They had not been communicating with spirits but were merely executing simple tricks, including the use of strings to manipulate objects and creating the illusion of supernatural occurrences. This revelation demonstrated the power of emotion and belief in fostering delusions to the extent that people even claimed to physically sense the presence of spirits.

Another notable account surrounds the Amityville Haunted House in New York, where a gruesome murder took place. The perpetrator of the heinous crime claimed that he had been influenced by ghostly voices in the house. Subsequently, another family, the Lutzes, moved into the same house and reported experiencing terrifying paranormal events. Their claims included sightings of ghosts and disturbing supernatural phenomena, ultimately compelling them to vacate the property. Nevertheless, investigative reports by ABC News later revealed that their accounts were fabricated. The murderer had lied in an attempt to evade legal consequences, while the Lutzes believed that by perpetuating these stories, they could secure lucrative book and film deals.

More recently, an incident in India came to the forefront involving an individual named Steve Huff, who asserted that he had established communication with the spirit of the late Bollywood actor, Sushant Singh Rajput. He recorded these interactions and posted them on YouTube, capitalizing on the emotional resonance of the actor's tragic passing. Numerous news outlets, including India TV, Amar Ujala TV, DNA, and News24, reported on these interactions as if they were genuine. However, an astute Instagram user unveiled the truth. Huff had extracted audio clips from an old interview with the actor, conducted by film critic Anupama Chopra, and manipulated them to create the illusion of communication with Sushant Singh Rajput's spirit.

In light of these instances where falsehoods were exposed, we must direct our attention to situations where individuals genuinely believe in their paranormal experiences. This brings us to films that purport to be "inspired by true events," such as the 2017 film "Veronica." This movie depicts a ritual involving a solar eclipse, during which the protagonist and her friends use an Ouija board to communicate with her deceased father and boyfriend, inadvertently summoning a malevolent entity. While the film claims inspiration from real events, the actual narrative derives from the story of a girl named Estefania. This real-life case garnered significant attention, with police reports even acknowledging paranormal activities at her home. When watching such films, one might be inclined to believe that some elements of truth are embedded within these narratives, particularly given the "inspired by true events" label. However, it is crucial to differentiate between being "based on true events" and "inspired by true events." When the director of "Veronica" was questioned, he clarified that the real story and the film's portrayal held substantial disparities. In actuality, the girl Estefania did not meet the same fate as her cinematic counterpart; she passed away several months later due to a medical condition. Moreover, there was a possibility that

Estefania suffered from an undiagnosed psychological disorder, a reality that could not be dismissed, given the limited medical resources available at the time in her rural locality.

In some cases, where entire families report paranormal experiences and ghostly encounters, a phenomenon known as Mass Psychogenic Illness or Shared Delusional Disorder may be at play. The notable Burari case, in which 11 family members tragically took their own lives in Delhi, serves as an illustrative example of this shared delusion. In this instance, the family believed that their actions would lead to salvation. Similarly, a family in Australia experienced shared delusional disorder while on a road trip, suspecting that they were being pursued by malevolent forces. Though they later reunited, the episode was attributed to shared delusion brought about by close emotional bonds and mutual reinforcement.

In conclusion, it is essential to maintain a rational perspective when exploring the realms of paranormal encounters and supernatural phenomena. While the allure of ghostly tales and inexplicable events is undeniable, scientific explanations, psychological phenomena, and shared delusions often underlie these stories. While enjoying such narratives for their entertainment value is entirely acceptable, it is crucial to approach claims of the paranormal with a discerning eye. The world of the supernatural is undoubtedly enticing, but the truths behind these claims often find their roots in the fields of psychology, science, and the human capacity for belief.

Subsequent to enduring seizures, it's essential to acknowledge that in the authentic account of Estefania, the possibility of an undiagnosed psychotic disorder cannot be dismissed. This potential disorder remained unaddressed due to the family residing in a rural locale during the 1990s when both technological and medical advancements were not as sophisticated as they are today. Furthermore, following Estefania's passing, her parents purportedly encountered paranormal phenomena, claiming to hear their daughter's cries. Yet, upon subjecting her mother to psychological examination, it became evident that her emotional instability, anxiety, and the desire for attention were the primary contributing factors. This level of detail is presented to elucidate a recurring pattern in cases of this nature. These incidents frequently serve as the inspiration for horror films. A common question arises: if even a single family member exhibits symptoms of a psychological ailment, but the entire family perceives and insists upon witnessing paranormal occurrences, how can this be explained?

In such situations, the phenomenon known as Mass Psychogenic Illness, or Shared Psychotic Disorder, comes into play. An illustrative example of this phenomenon is the well-known Burari Case, which involved the tragic mass suicide of 11 family members in Delhi (India). This case garnered substantial attention. An additional extraordinary occurrence took place within an Australian family, comprising five members, who embarked on a road trip. Suddenly, they succumbed to paranoia, believing that malevolent forces were plotting their demise. Subsequently, family members separated and went missing, only to reunite later. This scenario is recognized as a case of Shared Delusional Disorder (SDD), wherein individuals in close proximity mutually reinforce each other's delusions.

Now, transitioning to a different domain, let's delve into perplexing phenomena that are poised to astound you when you uncover their underlying mechanisms. First among these is the enigmatic Ouija board, spelled as O-U-I-J-A but pronounced as "wee-ja." These boards have made appearances in numerous films, including "The Exorcist," "Paranormal Activity," and "The Conjuring 2." Indian cinema has also featured them in productions like "A Death in the Goonj," as well as web series on platforms such as Zee5. Ouija boards are believed to serve as conduits for communicating with spirits. They typically feature alphabets, numbers, "yes," and "no," along with a triangular pointer referred to as a Planchette. To use these boards, individuals gather in dimly lit surroundings, often with candles, and beseech spirits to make contact. If a spirit is indeed present, they invite it to engage in communication. Participants then rest their hands on the Planchette and proceed to pose questions to the spirits. If the spirit wishes to convey a "yes" or "no" response, it is believed that their hands on the Planchette will involuntarily move toward the appropriate answer.

One intriguing aspect of this practice is the claim that participants do not consciously move their hands. While some individuals may engage in this activity for amusement, many genuinely believe that their hands are not moving of their own volition. Instead, they attribute this movement to the control of the spirits, perceiving it as a genuine interaction. How is this seemingly inexplicable phenomenon possible? The answer lies in a scientific concept known as the Ideomotor Effect.

The Ideomotor Effect represents a psychological phenomenon whereby individuals move their bodies unconsciously, without conscious awareness. For instance, one might experience the phenomenon of a hypnic jerk, in which the body moves suddenly just before falling asleep. In the case of Ouija boards, when participants believe the Planchette is moving independently, it is, in fact, their subconscious mind influencing their physical actions. Though they are unaware of it, their brains signal their bodies to carry out specific movements. To demonstrate this effect, one can conduct a simple Blindfold Test. If the Planchette were genuinely being moved by a spirit, participants who are blindfolded should consistently point to the correct answers. However, the reality is that when individuals are blindfolded and do not know the Planchette's position, they often produce random, nonsensical responses.

This same Ideomotor Effect is observed in people who claim to be possessed by spirits. Not all cases of possession are fraudulent. In some instances, individuals genuinely believe that they are possessed and exhibit corresponding behaviors. This belief may be influenced by their bodies moving involuntarily, without their conscious control. They interpret these movements as a sign of possession, as their bodies act beyond their own volition.

Likewise, some individuals assert that they possess the ability of automatic writing, enabling them to communicate with spirits.

However, when they engage in this practice, their subconscious mind may be guiding their hand movements without their conscious awareness.

It is essential to recognize that various scientific studies have explored and substantiated the Ideomotor Effect, offering empirical evidence for this psychological phenomenon. Thus, Ouija board sessions, claims of spirit possession, and instances of automatic writing can be elucidated by this scientific concept. While these phenomena may continue to intrigue and entertain those seeking thrilling stories, understanding their underlying psychological mechanisms can enhance one's critical perspective when encountering claims of paranormal experiences and otherworldly encounters.

Those who claim to have the ability to make their hands move for automatic writing are essentially demonstrating a comparable phenomenon. A significant portion of individuals making such assertions is undoubtedly being deceitful. Nevertheless, for those who genuinely believe in their abilities, they may be under the influence of the ideomotor effect, a concept we previously discussed.

Leaving the ideomotor effect aside, let's now scrutinize the practices of ghosthunters who employ advanced equipment in their pursuit of capturing paranormal entities. These ghosthunters often rely on infrared cameras to capture thermal patterns, which are then presented as what appears to be a negative photograph of spirits. In actuality, whenever there is a variation in temperature, an infrared camera can distinctly reveal this alteration. To illustrate this concept, consider sitting on a chair and generating some heat by rubbing your back against it. When viewed with an infrared camera afterward, it may appear as if someone is still seated on the chair. This visual effect arises from the residual heat present on the chair. A similar example can be observed when someone with wet feet exits a bathroom and leaves footprints on the floor. When these footprints are examined through an infrared camera, they may be interpreted as spectral footprints, as the temperature of the feet differs from the surrounding area.

Additionally, ghosthunters frequently employ an electromagnetic field (EMF) meter. This meter can react to the presence of electromagnetic waves emitted by various electronic devices such as cell phones, two-way radios, and other electronic equipment. Even minor electronic components like computer mouse devices or camera battery packs can cause fluctuations on the EMF meter. Motion sensor lights are also often used during ghost hunts. A mere passing mouse in an abandoned building can trigger these motion sensors, which are then wrongly attributed to sightings of spirits. The combination of these technical devices often results in the presentation of what many would consider nonsensical claims on television and in the media. This practice is not confined to any specific country but is prevalent in many nations. For example, a television show titled "Adhbut" on Aaj Tak broadcasts content branded as "Supernatural, Unimaginable, Unbelievable," which often includes the presentation of ghostly phenomena with VFX effects and eerie background music, accompanied by the host, Sweta Singh, narrating ghost stories.

While the entertainment value of such endeavors is unquestionable, it is crucial that they are unequivocally labeled as forms of entertainment. Watching horror films and enjoying the thrills they offer is a common pastime. The fear and suspense can provide a unique form of enjoyment. However, it becomes problematic when TV shows, films, or YouTubers assert with certainty that they have encountered and documented real ghosts, attempting to convince their audience of the existence of ghosts and spirits. This not only crosses ethical boundaries but also fosters superstition.

Regarding the Dimple Kapadia incident mentioned at the outset of this chapter, it is noteworthy that she was portraying a ghost in the film "Lekin." Her character was intrinsically linked to this role. When she reported her ghostly encounter, the response from Padmini Devi, the former princess, was that Dimple had spent the entire day filming in the role of a ghost. Thus, it was not uncommon for the character to linger in her thoughts, potentially leading to her perceived encounter with a ghost. Padmini Devi's explanation emphasized that Dimple had immersed herself in her character, and this immersion might have contributed to the illusion.

In conclusion, while the world of mysteries and paranormal phenomena offers captivating entertainment, it is imperative to maintain a discerning perspective. Enjoy these stories and experiences as entertainment, but be cautious about accepting them as proof of the existence of ghosts and spirits. Misleading the public by promoting superstition through false promises is ethically problematic, and it is essential to encourage critical thinking and skepticism when confronted with such claims.

15. Beyond Event Horizons: Demystifying Black Holes

Cast your memory back to 2014 when the world witnessed the release of a cinematic blockbuster directed by Christopher Nolan, "Interstellar." This film skillfully delved into space-related concepts, such as wormholes, black holes, and alien planets, all presented with scientific accuracy. However, one of the most awe-inspiring moments occurred at the film's climax, when the central character, Cooper, embarked on a perilous journey into a black hole. Within the narrative, the black hole was referred to as Gargantua. As Cooper ventured deeper into the black hole, he initially encountered nothing but an all-encompassing darkness. However, as he descended further, he discerned minuscule grain-like particles that pelted his spacecraft, resulting in visible scratches. These particles also generated flashes of light and sparks, eventually causing a conflagration aboard his craft. With no alternative, he ejected from his vessel and continued his descent into the black hole. Astonishingly, he found himself within a five-dimensional space—a mind-bending tesseract. In this extraordinary realm, he harnessed the power of gravity to communicate with his past self, crafting an unforgettable cinematic experience. Witnessing these scenes might have left you pondering their plausibility: Could such phenomena exist within a black hole? What would one encounter when plunging into a black hole? Today, we shall embark on a journey to comprehend these aspects.

The Enigma of Black Holes

"Black holes remained largely unknown until the 20th century. A black hole is a region in space where the force of gravity is so strong not even light can escape. From the outside, you can't tell what is inside a black hole. Black holes haunt our universe, dark centers of gravity that swallow everything in their path."

Einstein's Theory of Relativity

Our odyssey begins with the origins of the black hole's story, my dear friends. The history of black holes is relatively brief, as a mere century ago, these enigmatic entities remained shrouded in mystery. Their discovery was closely associated with Albert Einstein's revolutionary Theory of Relativity. This theory comprises two key components: the Special Theory of Relativity and the General Theory of Relativity.

Einstein unveiled the Special Theory of Relativity in 1905, shedding light on the intricate relationship between speed and time. When an individual travels in a spaceship at an exceptionally high velocity, the passage of time for them differs from those who remain on Earth. The swifter the spaceship's motion, the more time decelerates relative to individuals not onboard the ship. Notably, this time dilation is perceptible only when compared to people residing on Earth. The word "relative" plays a pivotal role here, as individuals within the spacecraft would not perceive time's slowdown, as it would appear to flow uniformly. It's only upon their return to Earth that they would detect a discernible time discrepancy. This phenomenon is termed "Kinematic Time Dilation".

However, it isn't solely speed that governs time dilation; gravity also plays a substantial role, as elaborated in Einstein's General Theory of Relativity, which he developed in 1915. According to this theory, the more intense the gravitational force one encounters, the greater the time dilation one experiences. This phenomenon is labeled "Gravitational Time Dilation." In the magnificent film "Interstellar," this principle was portrayed eloquently. When Cooper and his team descended onto the Aqua Planet, every hour spent there corresponded to seven Earth years, owing to the planet's close proximity to the gargantuan black hole, Gargantua. Thus, the black hole's immense gravitational force substantially influenced the passage of time.

To grasp this concept, Einstein encouraged us to envision space-time as a fabric, akin to a mesh, supporting celestial objects. The presence of these objects causes this space-time fabric to curve. This curvature not only augments the gravitational pull on physical entities but also leads to time dilation. Furthermore, the influence of gravity extends to other forms of energy, encompassing sound, heat, and light. Consequently, gravitational forces affect a multitude of phenomena, contrary to popular belief. This theory stipulates that certain objects in the cosmos can possess an immensely powerful gravitational force, capable of absorbing light entirely. These entities would thus appear completely black to observers because even light is incapable of escaping their grasp. These entities are precisely what we refer to as "black holes."

Intriguingly, Einstein did not anticipate the actual existence of black holes when he presented his Theory of General Relativity. Although he understood that gravitational forces influenced light, he did not seriously entertain the idea that such cosmic enigmas might truly exist. In fact, during his lifetime, the concept of black holes appeared rather outlandish to him. While the theory allowed for their theoretical existence, it also permitted concepts such as infinity, which were equally challenging to accept as practical realities. Thus, Einstein held reservations regarding the genuine existence of these phenomena. Remarkably, by the time of his passing, the term "black holes" had not even been coined.

A captivating tidbit of information pertains to Einstein's contention that light's speed imposes an upper limit on the influence of gravity. This means that gravity's effects are not instantaneously felt everywhere, but rather restricted by the speed of light. As a tangible example, envision the sudden disappearance of the sun. Remarkably, we would only become aware of this occurrence eight minutes later, as sunlight requires this amount of time to travel from the sun to Earth. Astonishingly, according to Einstein's theory, the gravitational consequences of the sun's vanishing would also manifest eight minutes later. This intriguing facet underscores the intricate relationship between the force of gravity and the propagation of light.

The Genesis of Black Holes
Even though the name "black hole" sounds undeniably sensational, it tends to engender a somewhat misleading impression. The term might inadvertently convey the notion of an actual "hole" existing in space. However, this is a fallacy, as black holes are not

openings or voids in the conventional sense. Rather, black holes are formed through the extraordinary life cycles of stars.

Indeed, my friends, there lies a central core within a black hole, but it's important to understand how this core comes into existence. Stars, including our very own Sun, engage in a perpetual nuclear fusion process within their core. These fusion reactions generate both heat and light. The heat, in particular, exerts an outward pressure. Simultaneously, at the core of the star, the force of gravity is pulling inwards. This equilibrium, characterized by the opposing forces, is what sustains the star throughout its life cycle. The energy derived from the nuclear fusion reactions prevents the star from collapsing under the weight of its own gravitational force.

However, these nuclear fusion reactions rely on a finite fuel source, typically either hydrogen or helium. Over time, this fuel gets consumed. When the star exhausts its fuel supply, the outward pressure ceases. With nothing to counteract the relentless gravitational pull, the star inevitably collapses upon itself. Please be aware that this process unfolds gradually; it's not an instantaneous occurrence. In fact, our very own Sun, with an anticipated lifespan of roughly 10 billion years, is expected to persist for quite some time.

Now, what transpires next hinges upon the mass of the star in question. To elucidate this, let's refer to a life cycle chart for stars.

Life Cycle of a Star

1. Small to Average-sized Star: If the star is relatively modest in mass, it undergoes a transformation into a Red Giant, and from there, it may evolve into a planetary nebula or a White Dwarf.

2. Huge Star with Considerable Mass: On the other hand, for massive stars endowed with substantial mass, once they've depleted their fuel reserves, they cool down and transition into Red Supergiants. Following this, the Supergiant undergoes a dramatic supernova explosion. After this cataclysmic event, a minuscule core

persists. If this core is compact, it's referred to as a Neutron Star. However, should the core exceed a certain size, it transforms into a Black Hole.

The fundamental concept is that when a star's mass undergoes gravitational collapse, it condenses to a remarkably diminutive size. To offer a tangible perspective, consider that if a star as large as our Sun were to transform into a black hole, the resultant black hole would possess a mere diameter of approximately 50 kilometers. Such a dramatic compression is truly astounding.

However, it's worth noting that our own Sun, often humorously referred to as our "son," will never mature into a black hole. This conclusion was substantiated by the celebrated Indian-American astrophysicist Subrahmanyan Chandrasekhar, who introduced the Chandrasekhar Limit. This limit posits that the maximum mass attainable for a White Dwarf is approximately 1.4 times the mass of our Sun. Beyond this threshold, White Dwarfs cannot maintain stability, subsequently transforming into either Neutron Stars or Black Holes. In the case of our Sun, it falls well below this limit, and thus, it is destined to culminate its stellar journey as a White Dwarf.

Understanding Black Holes
Having established why black holes exist, let's now delve into their characteristics and types. There are primarily three to four categories of black holes, my friends.

1. Stellar Black Hole: This is the most common type of black hole and is formed through the gravitational collapse of massive stars. It is estimated that within our Milky Way Galaxy, there are between 10 million to 1 billion such stellar black holes.

2. Primordial Black Hole: These black holes are a theoretical and somewhat mysterious category. They are presumed to possess a mass akin to that of a mountain, yet their dimensions are as minuscule as an atom. In essence, these black holes are purely hypothetical, with much remaining unknown about them.

3. Supermassive Black Hole: These are colossal black holes with a mass exceeding that of one million Suns combined. Remarkably, these mammoth entities can fit within a region no larger than our Solar System. Scientists speculate that at the core of major galaxies, including our Milky Way, supermassive black holes reside. The supermassive black hole situated at the heart of our galaxy is known as Sagittarius A*.

Additionally, there is ongoing speculation regarding a potential fourth type of black hole, although this remains unconfirmed. If it does indeed exist, this fourth category would be termed an "Intermediate Black Hole," bridging the gap between stellar and supermassive black holes. At present, no concrete evidence substantiates the existence of intermediate black holes.

Now, as depicted in films such as "Interstellar" and the remarkable images you may have encountered, it's vital to understand that black holes are not akin to colossal vacuum cleaners sucking in everything around them. Instead, they exhibit distinct features.

The Golden Ring around Black Hole

In these visual representations, black holes exhibit an orange-hued ring, known as an Accretion Disk, which encircles the central black hole. This accretion disk holds particular significance in the context of black holes. The stupendous gravitational force exerted by black holes draws gaseous matter and debris towards them, much like planets orbiting the Sun due to its gravitational pull. However, the gravitational influence of black holes is so intense that the matter in their vicinity attains tremendous speeds, becomes heated, and transforms into a fluid-like state. This matter takes on the appearance of fiery particles, with temperatures soaring to over a million degrees Celsius. As this matter ventures closer to the black hole, it orbits at even greater speeds, creating a visually striking accretion disk.

The particles orbit the black hole at such extraordinary speeds that they experience friction and compression, resulting in their luminosity. This emission consists predominantly of electromagnetic radiation, primarily in the form of X-rays. It's worth noting that although this accretion disk was accurately portrayed in the movie, there's a slight inaccuracy regarding its color. In actuality, human eyes cannot perceive X-rays, as they lie beyond the visible light spectrum. The orange-yellow color you often see in representations serves as a visual aid. The actual hue of this disk tends closer to blue. Even in the groundbreaking 2019 photograph of a black hole, the yellowish-orange coloration was employed to symbolize the accretion disk.

Another notable feature in the real image, which may not be as apparent in the cinematic portrayal, is that the particles on one side of the disk appear brighter than those on the other side. This distinction arises from the Doppler Beaming effect. By observing the authentic photograph of a black hole, you can discern the direction of the spinning particles. The brighter area corresponds to particles moving toward us, while the dimmer area indicates particles moving away. This effect is responsible for this contrast.

Returning to the cinematic representation, the accretion disk exhibits an intriguing optical illusion attributable to gravity. It creates the illusion that the disk envelops the upper and lower sections of the black hole. This illusion transpires because gravity warps the path of light. When observed from the front, the presence of the disk conceals the area behind it, and light from that concealed region must traverse the disk, influenced by gravity. This phenomenon leads to the perception that the disk encompasses the entire top and bottom of the black hole. However, when viewed from the top, black holes appear as conventional, round disks. This optical illusion is observable only when the black hole is viewed from the sides.

In addition to the accretion disk, as one ventures further into a black hole, a final circle of light known as the Photonsphere becomes visible. In this region, gravity's influence is so profound that light itself starts to orbit the black hole. And what is light composed of? Photons. These photons initiate an orbit around the black hole, theoretically making it possible for an observer inside this region to view the back of their own head, as light travels in a circular path, forming a ring.

Beyond this juncture lies the event horizon, marking the boundary of the black hole. It is considered a boundary because once crossed, the gravitational force becomes so overpowering that not even light can escape. Everything beyond this threshold is shrouded in utter darkness. Therefore, if an individual were to fall into a black hole and surpass the event horizon, theoretically, there would be no means of escape. After all, if even light succumbs to the inescapable clutches of a black hole, what chance would a human have? In the movie "Interstellar," it was depicted that Cooper's spacecraft continues its descent into a black hole, crosses this event horizon, and abruptly enters a five-dimensional space.

However, it's crucial to understand that this part of the film is a product of imaginative speculation. The interior of the event horizon remains a mystery because we lack concrete knowledge regarding its nature. The creators of "Interstellar" enlisted the expertise of a Nobel prize-winning physicist to ensure the scientific accuracy of their portrayal. Nonetheless, for aspects of the narrative that delve into the realm of the undiscovered, the film necessarily drew from imagination.

When contemplating the content within a black hole, one might turn to Einstein's General Theory of Relativity for insights. According to this theory, the central region of a black hole is referred to as a Singularity. This Singularity is the epicenter of the black hole, where the curvature of space-time becomes infinitely profound. To harken back to the metaphor of the mesh discussed earlier, the heavier the object, the more the space-time mesh bends. In the case of a black hole, this bending becomes so extreme that it stretches into infinite curvature. As per the theory of relativity, the influence of gravity on time, energy, and all other phenomena intensifies as gravitational force increases. With the escalating force of gravity, time slows down indefinitely. However, what does this mean when time slows down infinitely? Does it imply that if one ventures inside a black hole and somehow manages to depart, the external universe would have already met its end? This is a question to which we possess no definitive answer. We can merely speculate and construct theories. How do you envision it? Feel free to share your thoughts in the comments.

One intriguing theory posits that because light is absorbed upon entering the event horizon, inside this boundary, it may undergo multiple reflections before reaching the Singularity. As a result, certain elements inside the event horizon might indeed be visible. However, it's imperative to acknowledge that, thus far, the extent of our knowledge about black holes remains quite limited. Our practical understanding has been substantiated by a solitary photograph taken by the Event Horizon Telescope on April 10, 2019. This photographic evidence marked a monumental moment, confirming the existence of black holes more than a century after they were initially theorized.

One certainty regarding black holes is that should you fall into one, the gravitational forces at play would lead to your disintegration in a matter of milliseconds, rendering survival an impossibility. Nevertheless, there's no need for undue apprehension when it comes to black holes. In the past, many harbored misconceptions that black holes acted as cosmic vacuum cleaners, ceaselessly accumulating matter and eventually spelling doom for the entire universe. However, this isn't an accurate representation. As elucidated earlier, at the core of each galaxy, a supermassive black hole reigns, presiding over the orbits of all planetary bodies and stars within its gravitational purview. This arrangement is akin to the way all planets in our solar system orbit the Sun. Likewise, at the heart of each galaxy, albeit on a grander scale, supermassive black holes play a pivotal role in governing celestial motion.

In conclusion, by maintaining a safe distance from a black hole – akin to practicing social distancing – one can coexist without impending danger. As for the tantalizing concept of five-dimensional space alluded to in "Interstellar," it's a topic worth exploring in future.

Back in March 2003, the FBI apprehended a 44-year-old man named Andrew Carlssin. At that time, various newspapers were buzzing with reports about this individual's astonishing streak of luck. In the realm of stock markets, his success stood out like no other – a mere $800 investment had miraculously transformed into a staggering $350 million within a mere two weeks. Naturally, the FBI grew suspicious, suspecting that he might be engaged in a fraudulent scheme or insider trading.

During their questioning of Andrew, he provided an extraordinary explanation – he claimed to be a time traveler from 250 years in the future, armed with knowledge about stock market performances. This, he contended, was the source of his remarkable investment gains. The FBI, understandably, was taken aback by this assertion and firmly believed it to be a fabrication. As a result, they took it upon themselves to prove its falsity.

Upon closer examination, they discovered a perplexing detail – there was no record of Andrew Carlssin's existence prior to December 2002. Even more perplexing, on April 3rd, Carlssin was scheduled for a court appearance related to his bail, but he mysteriously vanished and was never located again. The question looms: was Andrew Carlssin a genuine time traveler? Is the idea of time travel scientifically plausible, or is it merely the stuff of fiction in books and movies?

In this chapter, we delve into the scientific underpinnings of time travel. The debate ensues as we ponder the possibility of a 'time machine.' The rules governing these temporal jumps are explored as we embark on a quest to understand the concept of time travel, which has intrigued us since the early 1900s.

In 1895, H.G. Wells penned his groundbreaking novel, 'The Time Machine,' which popularized the notion of a machine capable of propelling individuals into both the future and the past. Though Wells' work was unquestionably science fiction, it sparked the curiosity of numerous philosophers and physicists who delved into serious research on the topic, spawning a wealth of scholarly papers and an array of cinematic interpretations.

Time travel manifests in various forms in science fiction, and let's begin by examining some of these classifications. First, there is the one-way journey to the future, where individuals travel forward in time but cannot return. This is exemplified in movies like 'Interstellar,' where a time traveler ventures into the future while those they left behind continue to age and, in some instances, pass away.

Next is instantaneous time jumping, where a person can leap from one point in time to another instantly using a time machine, as seen in 'Back to the Future' and 'The Girl Who Leapt Through Time.' The third approach involves the time traveler standing still while time itself moves around them, as illustrated in 'Harry Potter and the Prisoner of Azkaban' when Hermione uses the time-turner.

In the case of slow time travel, depicted in the 2004 film 'Primer,' a time traveler enters a box and, for every minute they spend inside, they move back in time by a minute. So, to go back a day, they must remain inside the box for a full day. Lastly, there is the concept of traveling at the speed of light to traverse through time, as depicted in 'Superman' (1979) when the superhero exceeds the speed of light to journey back in time.

Among these varied concepts of time travel, the critical question arises: which methods could potentially be feasible in reality or the future? Which remain firmly grounded in scientific principles, and which might be deemed entirely unscientific and implausible? The answer may surprise you, as some of these notions, once relegated to the realm of science fiction, hold potential for actual realization even in the present day.

To broadly categorize time travel, there are two primary directions to consider – traveling into the future and venturing back into the past. First, let's explore the possibility of traveling to the future, a concept that finds its foundation in Albert Einstein's Theory of Special Relativity.

Einstein introduced the groundbreaking idea of time dilation, which challenged the previously held belief that time remains constant regardless of one's location or velocity. This notion was initially proposed by the renowned physicist Isaac Newton, who asserted that time was an immutable constant. However, Einstein boldly disputed this notion.

Einstein's analogy likened time to a river, where its flow could either slow down or accelerate, much like water in a river. This temporal fluctuation depended on factors such as speed and gravitational force. Astonishingly, Einstein posited that time could be manipulated — either accelerated or slowed down — by altering the speed and gravitational conditions of an object. This phenomenon is aptly known as time dilation.

Exploring the details of how Einstein arrived at this conclusion is a complex endeavor best reserved for another discussion, given its intricacies and depth. Nonetheless, time dilation can be categorized into two distinct mechanisms: one driven by speed and the other by gravity.

In the case of speed-induced time dilation, an object moving at a high velocity experiences a deceleration of time relative to a stationary observer. For a practical illustration, envision two clocks: one placed on the ground and another placed on an airplane. As the airplane accelerates to a high speed, the clock on board will begin to lag behind the stationary clock, illustrating the concept of Kinematic Time Dilation. This phenomenon has been substantiated through experiments employing atomic clocks to ensure precise time measurements.

Thus, as we unravel the scientific underpinnings of time travel, we find that the notion of traveling to the future is not relegated solely to the realm of science fiction. Albert Einstein's groundbreaking insights into time dilation reveal a pathway that enables time to be both sped up and slowed down, contingent upon speed and gravitational forces, opening a realm of possibilities for temporal exploration.

It was observed that the clock within the airplane lagged behind the other clock, a phenomenon demonstrated in the Hafele Keating Experiment. This experiment conclusively validated Einstein's theory of time dilation. Importantly, this doesn't imply that time itself is actually slowing down for the airplane's clock; rather, it underscores the relative nature of time. When we observe the airplane's clock from the ground, time appears to slow down in our perspective, creating a relative time differential.

For an individual on the airplane and the clock on board, time proceeds as it always has. To put it theoretically, if we were to construct a rocket capable of traveling at the speed of light and embarked on a ten-year journey at that speed, then returned to Earth, the time experienced on Earth would be 9,000 years ahead.

In simpler terms, traveling to the future is scientifically possible today, but the primary hindrance lies in the absence of an aircraft that can achieve such incredible speeds. Although reaching the speed of light is a challenge, advancements in technology offer hope for the development of aircraft and spaceships capable of attaining such velocities, potentially making time travel a reality.

Notably, Gennady Padalka, a Russian astronaut, holds the record for the most time traveled into the future, thanks to his extended stay in space—879 days, during which he maintained a speed of 28,000 kilometers per hour. This expedition caused him to age 0.02 seconds less than those on Earth, highlighting the potential for significant time travel in the future.

Apart from high-speed time dilation, Einstein's theory introduces another mechanism for time travel through gravitational force. The greater the gravity, the more pronounced the effect of time dilation. In this context, envision a fabric of space-time akin to a mesh with planetary objects represented as balls. Objects with more mass, and consequently more gravitational force, warp this mesh. Near an object with high gravitational force, time slows down considerably.

Consider spending time near Jupiter, the Sun, or even a black hole to experience slowed time. This phenomenon mirrors the concept seen in the movie 'Interstellar,' where each hour spent on a planet near a black hole equates to seven years for those not on the planet, a scientifically accurate representation.

While this elucidates the theoretical possibility of time travel into the future, the practicality of surviving near a black hole remains an open question. Black holes are known to possess immense mass and gravitational force, a reality confirmed when the Event Horizon Telescope captured the first-ever image of a black hole on April 10, 2019.

Returning to the subject of time travel, there are three distinct methods to journey into the future. The first is high-speed travel, the second involves proximity to a massive gravitational object, and the third is cryosleep. Cryosleep, depicted in films like 'Passengers,' places individuals in a state of suspended animation, halting the aging process. In reality, NASA is actively researching the development of stasis chambers, where astronauts can undergo mild hypothermia to conserve energy, slow down chemical reactions, and thus delay the aging process.

In a notable case from Japan, a man survived for 24 hours without sustenance or water, his body entering a form of hibernation at a temperature of only 22°C. This remarkable incident resulted in no permanent harm to his body, as his organs and brain remained unaffected. The concept of cryosleep is a promising area of research, and space agencies like NASA are actively exploring its potential applications.

We must adopt a wait-and-see approach for the time being. However, a noticeable aspect of the discussion so far is the exclusive focus on methods of traveling into the future. But what about journeys into the past? Is it a feasible endeavor in reality? At present, we cannot physically travel to the past, but we can gain insight into past events. This is because light takes a considerable amount of time to travel from one location to another. Even with its incredible speed, light requires years to reach certain destinations, quantified in light-years. If we were to arrive at a location before the light's arrival and observe it, we would effectively be witnessing the past.

However, this method allows for glimpses into the past rather than full-fledged time travel.

So, can we genuinely travel back in time? On June 28, 2009, the renowned physicist Stephen Hawking hosted a unique party at the University of Cambridge, complete with balloons and champagne. The intriguing aspect of this gathering was that, despite being an open invitation, not a single person attended. This social experiment was conceived to demonstrate the implausibility of time travel to the past. If it were possible, we should have been encountering time travelers from the future routinely. But this absence of such encounters raises serious doubts.

Theoretically, Einstein's theory of relativity doesn't rule out the prospect of traveling to the past. According to Einstein, if a gravitational force is exerted on the fabric of space-time, one powerful enough to create a wormhole, time travel into the past could become viable. This would necessitate an immensely potent gravitational field, akin to that of a black hole. A spinning black hole could potentially generate a gravitational force capable of bending space-time back on itself, forming a closed time-like curve known as CTC.

The practicality of this theoretical concept involves several challenges. Some theories posit that small wormholes spontaneously form and disappear in space, but they are exceedingly minuscule, smaller than atoms. To harness them for time travel, they would need to be enlarged, a task demanding substantial energy, including negative energy. Negative energy, an anti-gravitational force, would counteract the fabric of space-time, akin to the repulsion between like poles of magnets. This would be necessary to sustain the wormhole and make time travel possible.

However, the generation and application of negative energy remain theoretical and unproven at present. Nevertheless, this theory, proposed by a Nobel Prize-winning scientist, carries substantial weight and holds the potential for time travel to the past.

Yet, contemplating travel into the past reveals a host of formidable obstacles, chiefly paradoxes. One well-known example is the Grandfather Paradox. If one were to travel to the past and inadvertently prevent their great-grandfather's existence, it would disrupt the timeline and raise the question of how they were born in the first place. This paradox challenges the logical consistency of time travel. Several theories, including the Multiverse Theory, attempt to address these paradoxes by suggesting that changes in the past create new universes with distinct timelines.

Another intriguing paradox is the Predestination Paradox, which posits that our actions in the past inherently shape our present timeline. In this scenario, events are seemingly destined to unfold in a specific manner, despite attempts to alter the past. The outcome of any alteration becomes part of one's present reality.

Despite these fascinating theories, time travel into the past presents considerable challenges and raises questions of logical consistency. The potential for paradoxes may render it infeasible.

Conversely, time travel into the future is already scientifically feasible today and stands to become increasingly probable in the future. The means to glimpse the past are currently available, given the time it takes for light to traverse vast distances. This renders a form of time travel into the past plausible.

So, in a way, time travel already exists, and it aligns with the scientific concepts illustrated in films like "Interstellar." Yet, the story of Andrew Carlssin, as presented at the beginning of this chapter, is not rooted in reality. It was, in fact, a satirical narrative published in "The Weekly World News" that was later adopted and reported as fact by various media organizations. The tale is a fabrication, underscoring the importance of critical discernment in evaluating such stories.

17. The Red Plague Mystery: Birth of the First Vaccine

For over 3,000 years, a deadly virus wreaked havoc on Earth. The disease caused by this virus was excruciating and perilous, with a mortality rate of 30%. In other words, one out of every three infected individuals succumbed to its effects. Those who survived were left with permanent scars, particularly on their faces, which bore large blemishes. Tragically, many also suffered permanent blindness.

The devastating impact of this disease was seen when it swept through Japan in 1735, claiming the lives of a third of the population. When European colonizers introduced it to Mexico and America in the 1500s, it decimated 90% of the Native Tribal population. In the 18th century, one in every seven children born in Russia met their end due to this disease. It obliterated entire empires and civilizations from the annals of history. It's estimated that this virus claimed five million lives each year, totaling 500 million deaths in a century – half a billion people perished. In comparison, the recent Covid-19 pandemic pales in comparison.

Throughout history, this virus went by various names, including "Speckled Monster," "the Red Plague," and "Pox." In India, it was known as "Mata Lagna," meaning "Being afflicted by the Goddess." However, the most common name for this scourge was "Smallpox."

Interestingly, during the 1700s, a peculiar village in England appeared to be immune to this disease. The farmers living there seemed to possess an extraordinary defense against this deadly virus.

Smallpox is a viral disease caused by the Variola virus, classified as an Orthopox virus. Within the same category, one can find viruses like Monkeypox and Cowpox. Smallpox was exceptionally contagious, spreading readily through respiratory droplets from sneezes and coughs, saliva, and even contaminated surfaces, like towels and clothes used by infected individuals. Once infected, initial symptoms resembled a common cold, but soon, rashes would appear on the body, eventually turning into unsightly boils.

Around eight to sixteen days after infection, characterized by headaches, vomiting, rashes, and fever, death would occur. As previously mentioned, the mortality rate was 30%, significantly higher than that of Covid-19, which has a death rate of less than 1%.

One of the most disturbing aspects was its increased impact on children, who faced an even higher risk of death. The origins of this disease remain a mystery. It is believed to have emerged around 10,000 BC when humans transitioned to agriculture, coming into contact with animals such as cattle and poultry. These Orthopox viruses are naturally found in these animals, making zoonotic transmission a possible source. Some scientists even speculate that rodents could have played a role in the virus's spread.

The first recorded evidence of smallpox dates back to 1156 BC when an ancient Egyptian mummy was embalmed, displaying the characteristic facial scarring associated with smallpox. Ancient texts from India and China also make reference to the disease. In the Sanskrit text "Susruta Samhita," written around the 6th century BC, smallpox is described. Despite centuries of observation, modern medicine has yet to find a cure for this lethal disease.

Over time, people came to understand the concept of immunity through survival. Those who had previously battled the disease were less likely to be infected a second time. This led to the development of a practice known as inoculation, believed to have originated in India or China. In the 18th century, a group of Brahmins, called Tikadaar, would carry out inoculations, transferring scabs from infected individuals to healthy individuals via pricked skin. This method was a significant advancement in combating the disease.

However, there were drawbacks to this procedure. There was no guarantee that the small dose of the virus used for inoculation wouldn't be fatal. A 1%-2% death rate was associated with this method, yet it was still a more favorable option compared to the disease's 30% mortality rate. Additionally, those who were inoculated were left with permanent scars.

The third drawback was that the inoculated individuals could still spread the virus. Inoculation was indeed a double-edged sword.

In the 18th century, a peculiar event unfolded in the English village of Gloucestershire, where farmers, cattle breeders, and milkmaids seemed to possess immunity to smallpox. This phenomenon intrigued Dr. Edward Jenner, who embarked on an investigation to uncover the truth.

He discovered that those who had contracted Cowpox, a less severe disease, did not succumb to smallpox. This sparked a groundbreaking hypothesis – Cowpox might offer protection against smallpox. To test this theory, Dr. Jenner collected pus from a woman infected with Cowpox in 1796. This marked the beginning of his experiment, which would alter the course of medical history.

However, the pressing question was, on whom could he test this groundbreaking discovery? Someone had to serve as the host for this groundbreaking experiment. Dr. Jenner found a willing participant in his gardener's 8-year-old son, James. Without the ethical constraints and legal regulations of modern times, Dr. Jenner proceeded to intentionally infect young James with Cowpox. After a few days, the child developed a fever due to the Cowpox infection but, fortunately, he eventually recovered.

Dr. Jenner's next step was crucial. Six weeks later, he took lesions from a smallpox patient and intentionally infected young James with the smallpox virus. In contemporary society, conducting experiments on children in this manner is considered both morally reprehensible and illegal. However, the absence of such moral and legal standards during that era allowed Dr. Jenner to proceed. The intentional infection of a child with smallpox was a highly perilous endeavor, with a high likelihood of fatality. Nevertheless, young James emerged unscathed and had developed immunity against smallpox.

This groundbreaking experiment not only demonstrated the protective potential of cowpox against smallpox but also laid the foundation for the world's first vaccine. Dr. Jenner is credited with coining the term "vaccination," derived from the Latin word "Vacca," meaning cow. This term, originally associated with cowpox, has evolved to encompass a wide array of vaccines used today.

Vaccination was an immense leap forward in terms of safety compared to the earlier method of inoculation, which carried a 1%-2% risk of fatality. Cowpox, on the other hand, presented almost negligible risks of death. Today, the principles underlying this process are well-understood. Both cowpox and smallpox belong to the Orthopox virus family, and they are so similar that when a person's immune system is exposed to cowpox, it can effectively combat other similar viruses like smallpox, using the antibodies developed during the previous infection.

Recently, another orthopox virus, Monkeypox, has gained global attention. While it belongs to the same viral family, it is less severe than smallpox and less contagious. The death rate for Monkeypox is estimated to be around 3%-6%. Some studies suggest that the smallpox vaccine offers approximately 85% protection against Monkeypox. However, the emergence of a new disease always exerts a significant impact on society, particularly in terms of medical costs and expenses.

Returning to Dr. Jenner's remarkable contribution, one might assume that the world would have celebrated his groundbreaking discovery, recognizing that millions of lives could be saved. However, the reality was quite the opposite. Dr. Jenner faced severe backlash and widespread mockery. When he presented his findings to the Royal Society of London, his report was summarily rejected, with the President of the Royal Society advising him to abandon his research.

Nonetheless, Dr. Jenner persisted, conducting further research and collecting additional data. He published his book, titled "Enquiry Into The Causes And Effects of the Variolae Vaccinae." Over time, his work gradually gained acceptance among medical professionals and scientists, although convincing the general population proved to be an arduous task.

Many religious organizations opposed vaccination, contending that it defied God's plan and was unnatural. Some individuals were repulsed by the idea of their bodies being exposed to animal matter. Particularly in various European regions, there was a prevailing fear that vaccination would lead to individuals gradually transforming into cows. Painters and artists humorously depicted the emergence of bovine features from human bodies, contributing to the public's misconceptions.

Those who carried out inoculations were fervent opponents of vaccinations since it adversely affected their livelihoods. Over time, governments began to recognize the efficacy of vaccines, leading to mandatory vaccination policies. In 1853, England became the first country to enforce compulsory smallpox vaccination for children. This marked the beginning of the first Anti-Vax movements.

Despite these challenges, Dr. Jenner faced yet another formidable task – expanding the reach of vaccinations to the rest of the world. The key question was how to transport the vaccines, especially to countries where cowpox was not prevalent. Dr. Jenner devised three main methods to address this challenge.

The first method involved saturating a long string with pus from the vaccine and allowing it to dry before transporting it on ships. Healthy individuals would then make a small cut on themselves, ensuring it bled, and place the dried string on the bleeding wound. This method was instrumental in delivering the vaccine to Canada in 1800. However, it was not practical for long distances, as the strings became ineffective over time.

The second method entailed transporting the vaccine in glass tubes, sealed with wax. This approach enabled the delivery of the vaccine to other European countries and cities.

The third method, and perhaps the most unusual but successful, involved using children. Youngsters who were infected with cowpox were placed on ships and transported to distant locations. Their purpose was to infect more people in those areas with cowpox. The same ships also carried healthy individuals and doctors who would intentionally infect the unvaccinated population. By the time the ships reached their destination, a growing number of people had been vaccinated, ensuring that someone who had recently received the cowpox vaccine was always on hand.

The first cowpox vaccine in India arrived via the Middle East in 1802. Unfortunately, due to India's vast size and limited resources, the vaccine did not reach the masses, leading to a devastating smallpox outbreak in 1974. By 1977, the World Health Organization launched a global campaign to eradicate smallpox worldwide, championed by the Health Minister of the Soviet Union in 1958.

In the same year, the global program aimed at disseminating this vaccine worldwide was officially initiated. However, India posed a significant challenge in this endeavor. In 1962, the Indian government launched the National Smallpox Eradication Programme, investing substantial resources in vaccine manufacturing and health worker training. By 1966, approximately 60 million individuals had been vaccinated. Unfortunately, these efforts were insufficient, as the number of smallpox cases was steadily rising.

The most devastating smallpox epidemic in India occurred in 1974, claiming over 15,000 lives in just five months. At the time, India accounted for 86% of all smallpox cases worldwide. Several factors contributed to this alarming situation. India's vast population, characterized by constant migration for political, economic, and educational reasons, made it exceedingly challenging to reach every individual with vaccination information. Limited media penetration compounded the problem.

Furthermore, opposition to vaccination was fueled by superstition, as some believed that smallpox was a result of the goddess Shitala's anger. Instead of opting for vaccination, people chose to visit temples to appease the goddess. Religious beliefs and a widespread misconception that the vaccines were derived from cows led many to reject vaccination.

The vaccination process in the 1970s was notably painful, and the vaccines often spoiled due to India's hot climate. In 1970, the World Health Organization and the Indian government joined forces to develop a new plan for eradicating smallpox in India. This collaborative effort introduced freeze-dried vaccines that were easier to store and transport. Moreover, less painful vaccination techniques were introduced.

To educate and convince the population, a team of four WHO medical officers arrived in India in 1971, and an agreement was signed to acquire the new vaccines. These officers were deployed across the country to ensure that people, especially children, received this crucial vaccine. An extensive campaign was conducted, featuring posters and the active engagement of Prime Minister Indira Gandhi. Citizens were even offered a reward of ₹100 for reporting smallpox cases.

Radio broadcasts played a pivotal role in explaining the importance of vaccination to the public. Thanks to these combined efforts, in 1975, the last case of smallpox was reported in India. The disease was effectively eradicated from the country. Those born in or after 1975, their parents, or grandparents bear a round scar on their upper arm—a remnant of the smallpox vaccine.

The World Health Organization launched similar campaigns in Africa and South America, resulting in the last instance of natural smallpox infection in 1977 in Somalia. The last person to succumb to this disease was an English woman who was accidentally exposed to the virus in a laboratory in 1978. In 1979, the World Health Organization officially declared the global eradication of smallpox.

Since then, there has been no recorded case of smallpox in the world. If you are of my generation or were born after 1980, there's no need for a smallpox vaccine, as this virus has been eradicated worldwide. It's incredible to imagine that a small discovery by Dr. Jenner resulted in such profound positive changes. Each year, an estimated five million lives are saved due to the existence of this vaccine and the eradication of smallpox.

Regrettably, we still do not have a cure for this disease, although the need for one has ceased to exist. Instead, we prevented its spread through vaccination and ultimately eradicated it. Only two samples of the smallpox virus remain in the world, carefully stored in highly secure laboratories: one at the US Centre for Disease Control and Prevention and the other at the Russian State Research Center of Virology and Biotechnology. These samples are retained for the purpose of further research, with an underlying fear that genetic engineering could potentially revive this virus. Such an event could have devastating consequences if the virus were to escape from these laboratories and lead to another outbreak.

18. Rising Giants: The World of the Hindenburg Airship

On the evening of May 3, 1937, at approximately 8 PM, a majestic Hindenburg airship took off from Frankfurt, Germany, embarking on a journey across the Atlantic Ocean, destined for New Jersey, America. This grand airship accommodated around 97 passengers, comprising 36 passengers and 61 crew members. It's important to note that when I mention "aircraft" in this context, I am not referring to an airplane; rather, I'm referring to an airship. Hindenburg was indeed an airship, and not just any airship, but the world's largest one, measuring a staggering 245 meters in length. To grasp its enormity, one can compare it to a modern Boeing 747 aircraft, highlighting the remarkable scale of Hindenburg. Interestingly, it was only 24 meters shorter than the legendary Titanic, which was once the world's largest ship. This colossal airship earned the prestigious title of "Queen of the Skies" and was a source of immense pride for Nazi Germany.

The interior of the Hindenburg airship offered a luxurious experience to its passengers, characterized by opulence that is somewhat lost in today's air travel. Individuals enjoyed private sleeping quarters, a dedicated dining room where all could dine together, a splendid lounge featuring a grand piano, a space for reading and writing, and more. The ticket price for this extravagant journey was $700 at that time, equivalent to over $7,000 in today's currency. Consequently, only the wealthy elite could afford to travel in such lavish comfort.

After a three-day journey, on May 6, 1937, the Hindenburg reached its destination in America, thousands of miles from its departure point. It was scheduled to land at Lakehurst Naval Air Station in New Jersey, and the descent began around 7 PM. The landing procedure was unique, involving ground personnel who held onto the airship's ropes. Crowds had gathered to witness this historic moment, as the landing was being filmed that day. Unfortunately, the weather conditions were less than favorable, with overcast skies, clouds, and strong winds. In an effort to align the airship with the wind direction, the captain executed a sharp turn, while the ground crew hastened to secure the ropes. Tragically, at that critical moment, a deafening explosion resonated through the air, and in the blink of an eye, the Hindenburg airship was engulfed in flames. Within a mere 34 seconds, the once-mighty airship was reduced to smoldering wreckage.

"The actual crash of the Hindenburg, an airship destroyed in less than half a minute, seared in the skeleton of what was once a mighty airship."

The Hindenburg disaster sent shockwaves around the world, prompting intense scrutiny to ascertain the cause of this catastrophe. Experts and investigators explored three primary theories. The first theory posited that the airship was deliberately sabotaged, part of a sinister plot to destroy the pride of Nazi Germany. This perspective suggested that either anti-Nazi activists or a foreign nation had concealed a bomb within the Hindenburg, leading to the sudden explosion. Some even speculated that Adolf Hitler himself had orchestrated the explosion, with a bomb planted on the airship to undermine its legacy. This theory was rooted in the complex relationship between Hugo Eckener, the owner of the airship company, and Hitler's regime. Eckener was one of the few who openly opposed Hitler and the Nazis during their reign, a perilous stance during that time. In 1933, when the Nazi party ascended to power, Hitler attempted to arrest Hugo Eckener, but this arrest was thwarted by then-German President Paul von Hindenburg. Incidentally, the airship was christened with the name "Hindenburg" in honor of the president. Three years later, in 1936, when the world's largest airship was ready for service, Hitler's propaganda minister, Joseph Goebbels, urged Eckener to name it after Hitler. Eckener, however, staunchly resisted, and instead, he named it Hindenburg. This choice was viewed by some as a deliberate affront to Hitler, and consequently, some believed that Hitler had resorted to bombing the airship to discredit Eckener and his legacy.

The second theory emphasized static electricity generated by the airship in the atmosphere. This theory proposed that a static charge accumulated on Hindenburg's metal frame, and when it sparked, it ignited the hydrogen gas within the airship, resulting in the explosion. It was suggested that the sharp turn executed by the pilot may have contributed to the disaster.

The third theory centered on the possibility of a lightning strike. Given the unfavorable weather conditions, with stormy skies and clouds, some speculated that a lightning strike could have ignited the hydrogen gas, leading to the fiery disaster.

So, which theory holds the most credibility? To discern the answer, it's vital to delve into the history of airships. Nowadays, flying is a routine part of life, thanks to airplanes. However, if we journey back 500 years, we find that people could only dream of flying. In the 1500s, individuals gazing upon soaring birds in the sky harbored a profound desire to take flight themselves. This ambition led to numerous attempts at human flight, often involving leaps from towers, high walls, and imaginative solutions such as attaching feathers, kites, or balloons to achieve liftoff. Over time, people came to realize that there were primarily two methods for achieving human flight. The first method involved becoming lighter than air.

Just like a hot air balloon. The second approach requires generating sufficient power to enable flight in the sky, and being lighter than air is not a prerequisite. This method is employed by all the airplanes and helicopters you observe soaring through the skies today. These aircraft generate the requisite power to navigate the air. However, the narrative of airships is rooted in the first method, which entails becoming lighter than air. In the 1770s, two innovative and intelligent brothers in France, Joseph-Michel and Jacques-Étienne Montgolfier, stumbled upon the concept that ignited the era of air travel.

One day, Joseph was captivated by the sight of clothes being dried over an open flame. He observed how the heat from the fire caused the clothes to ascend into the air. This inspired him to ponder the possibilities on a grander scale. He began by constructing a small box crafted from thin wood and draped in a lightweight cloth. Inside this box, he placed a crumpled piece of paper, which he then set ablaze. To his amazement, the box ascended once the fire was ignited. Promptly, he embarked on the construction of a larger model of the box in collaboration with his brother. On December 14, 1782, the first full-scale model was subjected to a test flight. Wool and hay were set on fire to achieve lift, and the resulting lifting force was so powerful that they lost control of the box, which continued to soar for 2 kilometers. The following year, in 1783, a public demonstration was staged at the palace of King Louis in Versailles, France. During this spectacle, a duck and a hen were placed inside the box to illustrate the safety of flight for animals. The king was sufficiently impressed, leading to the granting of permission for human passengers. Thus, the hot air balloon was born, with Jacques-Étienne Montgolfier becoming the first human to take flight in such a craft.

Advancing the narrative to the 1850s, in a small German town, lived a young boy bearing the name Ferdinand Adolf Heinrich August Graf von Zeppelin, a name of considerable distinction. This boy ventured to America during the American Civil War, where he observed the use of balloons by the Union Army. This experience piqued his fascination with balloons, and he ascended through the ranks of the army, eventually penning the idea of an airship in his diary in 1874. By that time, balloons had seen considerable advancements, with the installation of engines enabling controlled navigation. Some balloons utilized steam engines, while others relied on electric-powered engines. In 1891, at the age of 52, Zeppelin resigned from the military and devoted himself entirely to the development of airships. His concept was to use multiple gas bags in a single airship to enhance rigidity and create a substantial and durable aircraft. Zeppelin collaborated with a team of engineers to refine this idea and constructed an aluminum framework.

In 1898, with some financial backing, he completed the first airship, known as LZ-1. To this day, airships are often referred to as "Zeppelins" in honor of the man who pioneered them, Ferdinand Adolf Heinrich August Graf von Zeppelin. Nevertheless, the path forward was fraught with numerous challenges. Zeppelins primarily utilized hydrogen gas for buoyancy, whereas in the United States, helium gas was employed. The distinction between these two gases is significant; hydrogen is highly flammable, whereas helium is inert and does not readily catch fire. In terms of function, both gases are lighter than air, enabling the airship to remain aloft. On July 2, 1900, LZ-1 completed its first successful flight, remaining airborne for 20 minutes despite sustaining damage upon landing.

Zeppelin initiated repairs, but due to a shortage of funds, he resorted to mortgaging his wife's assets to secure additional capital. In 1905, LZ-2 was constructed; however, before it could take flight, a control component broke off, rendering it immobile. Restoration took another year. In 1906, Zeppelin subjected it to testing once more, revealing another significant flaw: the airship lost control due to strong winds. The salvageable components were used to build LZ-3, which aimed to demonstrate to the military that a successful aircraft could be constructed. The military, however, stipulated that the airship needed to endure flight for a minimum of 24 hours to pass a durability test. Regrettably, LZ-3 failed this test.

To meet the military's requirements, Zeppelin developed LZ-4; however, during a storm, LZ-4 was utterly destroyed. In a high wind scenario, the Zeppelin broke free from its moorings and ultimately exploded. The story embodies the real-life adage: "Try, try until you succeed." Perseverance is the key; those who persist in their efforts are never truly defeated. Simultaneously, in 1903, the Wright brothers achieved their first successful flight in an airplane, a story rich in historical significance.

Despite numerous setbacks, Zeppelin began to gain public attention, drawing recognition for his unwavering dedication to airship development. This led to increased investments, culminating in the establishment of his own company. Significant improvements were made to LZ-3, and in 1908, successful test flights were conducted despite adverse weather conditions. LZ-3 was officially embraced by the government, marking a momentous achievement for Zeppelin and earning him considerable acclaim. Over the following years, Zeppelin continued to refine his designs, but sadly, he passed away in 1917.

Following the conclusion of World War I in 1918 and the signing of the Treaty of Versailles, Germany found itself prohibited from retaining military aircraft. Up until this point, airships had primarily been employed for military purposes. This is where Dr. Hugo Eckener steps into our narrative. After Ferdinand von Zeppelin's passing, Eckener assumed control of the company. He was the first to recognize that Zeppelins could serve a dual purpose - not only for military applications but also for commercial flights.

In 1924, LZ-126 embarked on its maiden voyage, with none other than Hugo Eckener himself at the helm. It completed a journey spanning over 8000 kilometers in a mere 80 hours. Upon its arrival in America, it was warmly received, and people hailed it as an "Angel of Peace." This was a significant transformation, where a machine once exclusively associated with warfare was now being utilized for civilian purposes.

Eckener went on to develop the next model, LZ-127, in 1928. Regrettably, the era of airships was not destined to endure for long. As I previously mentioned, the Nazi Party ascended to power in 1933, and Eckener was one of the few individuals who openly criticized Adolf Hitler's regime.

Returning to the time after the Hindenburg disaster, an investigation spanning several decades determined that neither Hitler nor the Nazi Party were responsible for the catastrophe. The prevailing theory behind the accident points to hydrogen leakage and the resulting explosion due to static electricity. Sadly, this disaster severely tarnished the reputation of airships, highlighting the volatility of hydrogen. Traveling in airships was perceived as a hazardous undertaking, even though helium gas was also an option. The problem, however, was that helium gas was predominantly restricted to the United States, which had imposed an export ban on it.

By the 1940s, while the prestige of airships waned, with the public becoming increasingly wary of air travel in them, airplane technology was rapidly advancing. Passenger planes were demonstrating substantial improvements in terms of speed, reliability, and operating costs. Airplanes were flying at speeds between 700 and 1,000 kilometers per hour, far surpassing the approximately 100 kilometers per hour speed of airships. Obtaining helium gas remained a challenge, and airships were more vulnerable in adverse weather conditions.

Regrettably, individuals of our generation neither had the opportunity to travel in airships nor witness them firsthand. This is unfortunate, as the experience of airship travel was notably distinctive. Traveling at low altitudes with large windows must have provided a breathtaking view. Fortunately, there is the potential for an airship revival in the coming years.

In 2017, a UK-based company, Hybrid Air Vehicles, conducted a test flight for their colossal airship, the Airlander 10, which is recognized as the world's largest aircraft. Today, acquiring helium gas is less problematic, rendering airship travel safer. Furthermore, due to growing concerns about carbon emissions linked to climate change, airships release only one-tenth of the carbon emissions compared to airplanes. They are also more fuel-efficient and fly almost silently, generating minimal noise pollution. As per the company, they anticipate launching commercial airship flights after 2030. How this resurgence unfolds remains to be seen.

19. Submersible Secrets: Unraveling the Titan Submarine

On the 18th of June in the year 2023, at precisely 9:30 in the morning, a group of five adventurous souls embarked on a unique and daring voyage in a submersible vessel known as Titan. Their mission: to delve deep into the ocean's abyss and explore the wreckage of the fabled Titanic, a ship with an illustrious history that had met its watery demise approximately a century earlier.

This form of adventure tourism is not for the faint of heart and comes at a considerable cost. Each passenger aboard the Titan had invested over ₹20 million for the privilege of a few hours on this extraordinary journey. The steep price tag reflects the daunting task of reaching the Titanic's resting place, which is concealed beneath the sea's surface at a staggering depth of 3,810 meters, or roughly 12,500 feet.

The submarine initiated its descent, a journey that would span approximately two hours before reaching the depths of 3,810 meters. At 15-minute intervals, the submersible maintained its sole means of communication with the surface world by transmitting signals to its support vessel, the Polar Prince, stationed above. On that fateful day of the 18th of June, just 1 hour and 45 minutes into the submersible's aquatic exploration, an unexpected and perplexing event occurred: it lost all contact with the Polar Prince.

By 4:30 in the afternoon, the scheduled time for the Titan's return from its subaquatic odyssey had come and gone without a trace. As evening drew near, at precisely 7:10 PM, the crew aboard the Polar Prince made the crucial decision to alert the US Coast Guard. This marked the inception of a four-day-long, multinational search and rescue operation of unprecedented scale aimed at locating the lost submersible. The mission engaged a multitude of assets, including aircraft, maritime vessels, and robotic devices, all deployed in a relentless quest for answers. At the forefront of everyone's thoughts loomed a single, burning question: What had transpired within the depths of the ocean, and what had become of the five intrepid passengers aboard the Titan?

As per reports from the US Coast Guard, the remnants of the Titan were eventually recovered from the ocean floor, attesting to a catastrophic loss of the pressure chamber. Amid the wreckage, the story of the Titan Submersible began to unravel.

The vanishing act unfolded in the expansive Atlantic Ocean, located in close proximity to Canada, approximately 600 kilometers from Newfoundland, a Canadian island. At this site, shrouded in the ocean's depths, lies the fragmented remnants of the Titanic, with its bow and stern resting at a distance of about 800 meters apart from each other.

It is crucial to note a fundamental distinction between submarines and submersibles. Submarines possess their own propulsion systems, enabling them to autonomously traverse the ocean and resurface at will. In contrast, submersibles are reliant upon a surface support ship for their deployment and recovery. In the case of the Titan Submersible, this role was undertaken by the Polar Prince, situated on the ocean's surface, orchestrating the entire mission.

The mastermind behind this ambitious venture was OceanGate, a company helmed by CEO Stockton Rush, a seasoned aerospace engineer by trade. In 2009, Rush established OceanGate, a private enterprise dedicated to offering affluent individuals the opportunity to partake in deep-sea expeditions for tourism purposes. OceanGate expanded its offerings in July 2021 to include Titanic tours, which were preceded by expeditions to various shipwrecks and maritime sites. At present, OceanGate maintains a standing as a pioneer in the field of underwater exploration.

Titan, the submersible of interest, was not the sole vessel in OceanGate's fleet. The company also boasted two additional submersibles, Antipodes and Cyclops, each equipped with unique capabilities suited to different underwater depths. While Antipodes was engineered for submersion to depths of up to 304 meters, Cyclops was capable of venturing down to 500 meters. In contrast, Titan was the standout among them, designed to withstand the crushing depths of 4,000 meters, or 4 kilometers beneath the ocean's surface. This exceptional depth-seeking capability made Titan the ideal choice for journeying to the Titanic wreck itself.

Visualizing the staggering depth of 3,800 meters, consider the following chart generated by The Washington Post, with measurements in feet. For perspective, an average adult male's height is approximately 6 feet. The iceberg that infamously collided with the Titanic extended approximately 100 feet above the water's surface, with a substantially greater underwater presence. Recreational scuba divers typically explore depths no greater than 130 feet. Beyond this point, a twilight zone begins where only a limited amount of light reaches. Notably, the deepest underwater rescue operation to date took place at a depth of 1,600 feet.

At the depth of 2,600 feet, the eerie habitat of giant squids begins, with these enigmatic creatures thriving in the depths of the ocean. The ambiance in this realm often evokes the sensation of an alien world. Progressing further to the abyssal depths, spanning 5,000 feet, 6,000 feet, 8,000 feet, 10,000 feet, and eventually culminating at 12,500 feet, one reaches the ocean floor, where the Titanic's wreckage lies in perpetual rest. At this crushing depth, the water pressure exceeds surface levels by nearly 400 times, requiring meticulous design and engineering to ensure the safety of any submersible venturing to such depths.

Moreover, the Titan submersible featured an expansive viewport, which is the observation window that allows passengers to gaze upon the underwater world. It was lauded as the largest viewport ever installed on a private submersible. Despite its formidable capabilities, the Titan could accommodate only five occupants, with its hull constructed primarily from carbon fiber, a lightweight yet robust material.

Two titanium caps adorned its extremities, while its total length extended to approximately 6.7 meters, bearing a weight that exceeded a staggering 10,400 kilograms. The design of this remarkable contraption featured four electric thrusters on its exterior – two horizontal and two vertical – which facilitated its maneuverability in the depths of the ocean.

Notably, the Titan submersible was operated using a video game controller, an intriguing facet of its functioning. This might seem unusual, but even the US Navy employs Xbox controllers to manage their submarines and periscopes. In the case of the Titan, this controller was the primary interface for the pilot navigating the submersible beneath the waves.

Internally, the submersible lacked traditional seating arrangements but included a compact restroom situated adjacent to a viewport. A notable quirk was the absence of any partition around the restroom, necessitating that passengers turn away or engage with a television screen if the facilities were in use. Despite its utilitarian design, the Titan submersible provided an exclusive vantage point for its occupants to witness the subaquatic world.

Given their profound submersion into the ocean's depths, traditional GPS technology was rendered ineffective. Communication with their surface support ship was reliant on a text messaging system, though details regarding the available internet connection remain unclear. A tweet from OceanGate alluded to the use of Starlink's satellite internet service for communication.

Returning to the events of the 18th of June, the Titan submersible embarked on its journey with a total of five individuals on board. Among them, the first was 58-year-old British billionaire, Hamish Harding, celebrated for his adventurous spirit and status as a three-time Guinness World Record holder. His remarkable feats included a journey to the South Pole alongside astronaut Buzz Aldrin in 2016, a four-hour dive into the Mariana Trench's deepest part, and participation in Blue Origin's suborbital flight initiated by Jeff Bezos' space exploration company.

The second passenger was Paul Henri Nargeolet, a 77-year-old retired commander from the French Navy. Notably, he had visited the Titanic wreck 37 times and held the position of Director of Underwater Research for the RMS Titanic project.

The third and fourth passengers were Shahzada Dawood, a British-Pakistani businessman, and his 19-year-old son, Suleman. Shahzada was the owner of one of Pakistan's most prominent companies, and Suleman accompanied his father on the journey despite harboring apprehensions.

On the day of the expedition, the Titan submersible maintained a communication link with the support ship at 15-minute intervals. However, this connection was abruptly severed at 11:15 AM, and subsequent attempts to reestablish contact proved futile. Nevertheless, the expectation remained that the Titan would resurface at the scheduled time of 4:30 PM, as it was equipped with mechanisms allowing passengers to manipulate it from within by adjusting ballasts. These ballasts, weighty components within the submersible, are fundamental to maintaining stability and controlling buoyancy. Their removal permits a submersible to ascend in the water.

At 4:30 PM, when the Titan failed to emerge from the depths, the crew aboard the support ship initiated a period of waiting before ultimately notifying the US Coast Guard at 7:10 PM. A frenzied and time-sensitive search operation ensued, recognizing that the Titan's life-support systems carried only four days' worth of oxygen. This scant supply left a narrow window for any potential rescue operation. Unfortunately, no emergency locator beacon (Emergency Position Indicating Radio Beacon, EPIRB) was installed on the submersible, complicating search and retrieval efforts.

Moreover, even if the Titan had surfaced, passengers would have been at risk due to a lack of external access, as the submersible's hatch could only be sealed and unsealed from the outside. To compound matters, the search area spanned a vast 25,000 square kilometers, presenting a formidable challenge. The area was roughly seven times the size of India's state of Goa, underscoring the difficulty of locating a van-sized submersible.

Efforts to rescue the passengers were further hindered by the fact that the deepest recorded underwater rescue, conducted in 1973, reached a depth of only 480 meters. Despite the overwhelming odds, multiple aircraft and ships, supported by remotely operated vehicles (ROVs), were mobilized in the search operation. ROVs are robotic vehicles operated from the water's surface, capable of descending into the depths to locate and retrieve objects. In total, three ROVs were deployed in the quest to locate the Titan.

After three days of search efforts, an unexpected breakthrough occurred on the third day when a sonar on a Canadian aircraft detected peculiar sounds resembling knocking or banging at half-hour intervals. These sounds were subsequently verified by the US Coast Guard. On the 22nd of June, an ROV scouring the ocean floor stumbled upon fragments of the submersible, situated approximately 490 meters from the Titanic's bow. These discoveries confirmed that the Titan had met a tragic fate, with no hope of rescuing its passengers, who had sadly perished within its confines.

On that very day, the US Coast Guard convened a press conference to clarify that the banging sounds they had previously detected had no bearing on the Titan submersible. Instead, the prevailing consensus pointed to a different and dire conclusion: the Titan had suffered implosion due to extreme pressure. It's essential to recognize that implosion represents the contrary of an explosion; whereas an explosion entails an outward release of force, implosion involves a force that compresses inward. In the case of catastrophic implosion, the process transpires with such speed that the entire structure disintegrates virtually instantaneously, resulting in an almost imperceptible end for those within.

The primary inquiry centers on the underlying cause of this catastrophic implosion. The Titan's central structure, as mentioned earlier, was constructed from carbon fiber, an experimental choice unlike the more conventional materials like steel, titanium, or aluminum typically used in the construction of submarines and submersibles. Evidently, the tragic fate of the Titan indicates that carbon fiber is ill-suited for such deep-sea endeavors. Renowned ocean explorer Robert Ballard, who discovered the Titanic wreck in 1985, commented that they had conducted thousands of dives utilizing various vehicles to reach the ocean's depths, never once experiencing a vehicle loss until this catastrophic incident.

James Cameron, the celebrated director of iconic films like "Titanic" and "Avatar," who had undertaken multiple deep-sea expeditions, echoed Ballard's sentiments. Both experts conveyed that it is statistically safer to navigate a vessel like Alvin than drive along Interstate 95.

Remarkably, the titanium caps at either end of the submersible survived unscathed on the seabed, contrasting starkly with the disintegrated state of the main carbon fiber body. This led to substantial criticism of the Titan's safety measures. Old interviews featuring the CEO of OceanGate, the company behind the Titan submersible, frequently echoed a sentiment that cast safety regulations as excessive.

In a 2019 interview, he expressed frustration with the US Passenger Vessel Safety Act of 1993, which he felt prioritized passenger safety at the expense of commercial innovation. He deemed it superfluous and advocated for a more relaxed approach to safety. In a separate interview the following year, he controversially opined, "At some point, safety just is pure waste. I mean, if you just want to be safe, don't get out of bed, don't get in your car, don't do anything."

In his own words, "I've broken some rules to make Titan. I think I've broken them with logic and good engineering behind me," referring to his intentional disregard of the rule prohibiting the use of carbon fiber and titanium.

The disregard for safety came under the spotlight when, in January 2018, OceanGate's Director of Marine Operations, David Lochridge, voiced significant safety concerns regarding the Titan submersible. When these concerns went unaddressed, he resorted to legal action, emphasizing the necessity for a safety assessment and certification, which OceanGate declined to undertake. The legal dispute eventually concluded in 2018.

However, on March 27, 2018, 36 prominent figures from the field of deep-sea exploration, including industry leaders, oceanographers, and seasoned ocean explorers, penned a letter to Stockton Rush, the CEO of OceanGate. The letter implored him to exercise caution in the pursuit of safety, emphasizing that the experimental approach and lack of quality checks could potentially lead to a catastrophic accident.

In March 2018, another specialist in deep-sea exploration cautioned the CEO via email to adopt a more conservative approach to safety, highlighting the grave dangers faced by Rush and his clients. Throughout the race to reach the Titanic, Rush was accused of repeating a phrase synonymous with perilous overconfidence: "She is unsinkable."

This tragic episode has now etched the name of Stockton Rush into history alongside other inventors who met their fate through their own creations, underscoring the irreplaceable significance of safety standards and regulations. It serves as a stark reminder that overlooking these safeguards can lead to disastrous outcomes.

20. Cryptic Ciphers: Deciphering Cicada 3301

On January 4, 2012, an enigmatic user on 4chan, identified only by the cryptic pseudonym 3301, unveiled an image on the infamous /b/ board, initiating one of the most elaborate and puzzling scavenger hunts in the history of the internet. What transpired in the following years left the online community both fascinated and perplexed, as Cicada 3301 challenged users to uncover a series of mind-bending puzzles, sparking rumors of secret societies, intelligence agencies, and recruitment for highly skilled individuals.

The mysterious image concealed a message, and what followed was an intricate web of encrypted codes, leading to yet another image. A string of decipherable text was discovered by users who opened the image with a text editor. This text contained a cipher that, once decoded, unveiled a link to the next challenge. While this appeared to be a dead-end, users utilized an application known as OutGuess to extract hidden information from the image.

The extracted data led to a subreddit, which held clues to a book and a code. Solving this puzzle unveiled a phone number, leading to a prerecorded message. This initiation sparked a community of armchair detectives eager to solve the puzzle, yet the purpose and origin of Cicada 3301 remained a mystery.

Speculation arose, with some dismissing it as an elaborate prank and others considering the complexity as evidence of something more profound. Rumors suggested the involvement of a secret society or intelligence agency seeking individuals proficient in cryptography and related fields. Despite these speculations, the true nature of Cicada's purpose remained unknown.

The puzzle extended to the physical world, as coordinates unveiled locations around the globe. Fourteen locations across five countries were marked, prompting participants to venture outdoors. This reinforced the belief that Cicada might be the work of a formidable international collective. At each location, posters featuring the cicada symbol and a QR code were discovered, further deepening the mystery.

Participants unlocked the puzzle's next stages by solving riddles contained within the QR codes, leading to books and websites. The puzzle's culmination took an unexpected turn when a select group of first arrivals were granted access to a private final stage. The puzzle's end was marked by a message: "We want the best, not the followers." Finalists were advised against collaboration and sharing details of this confidential stage.

After a month of silence, an image on the subreddit announced the puzzle's conclusion. Cicada had seemingly identified the "highly intelligent individuals" they sought, leaving many questions unanswered. The lack of explanation left some convinced that the entire journey was an elaborate wild-goose chase.

A year later, on January 5, an image carrying a PGP signature was posted, indicating the return of Cicada 3301. The PGP signature served as a means of authentication, ensuring the legitimacy of clues. After a year of imitations, this image finally matched the official PGP signature, reigniting the puzzle.

The second puzzle closely resembled the first, guiding participants through messages, books, recordings, and the discovery of a cryptic Twitter account. A runic alphabet added an extra layer of intrigue. Coordinates led participants to eight locations in four countries, replicating the physical hunt of the first puzzle. However, the second puzzle diverged from the first as it did not conclude with an official message from Cicada.

In 2014, Cicada 3301 unveiled its third puzzle, maintaining its tradition of using cryptic images to kick-start the challenge. Participants deciphered messages that led them to a peculiar book titled "Liber Primus," written primarily in runes. While the translated pages contained philosophical and ideological content akin to a manifesto, the encrypted runes concealed deeper mysteries. Cicada's intent with this book puzzle remained elusive, with some likening the writings to those of a cult.

"Liber Primus" presented numerous clues and codes, pointing to hidden websites on the deep web, which participants have struggled to locate. A recording titled "Interconnectedness" added to the enigma. Despite efforts, many pages in the book remain untranslated, buried beneath layers of encryption.

As 2015 came and went without the launch of a new puzzle, it became evident that "Liber Primus" might hold the key to Cicada's return. The group's silence left many questions unanswered:

1. What is the true purpose of these puzzles?
2. Who is behind Cicada 3301?
3. What lies at the end of this cryptic journey?

The End:
In Cicada's early days, some speculated that it might be an alternate reality game (ARG) orchestrated by a corporation to promote a product or service. However, subsequent puzzles and the absence of commercialization have dispelled this notion. Leaked information from the private end-stage of each puzzle suggests that Cicada may be a group with a mission aligned with privacy and security principles.

For example, an email allegedly sent to finalists at the conclusion of the first puzzle described Cicada as an international group advocating privacy as an inalienable right. They aimed to recruit like-minded individuals to develop privacy-conscious solutions.

The lack of a PGP signature in the email's leaked version raised questions about its authenticity. Despite this uncertainty, the idea of a secret society recruiting through cryptographic puzzles isn't unprecedented. Governments and corporations have used similar recruitment techniques in the past.

What about the recruits who were chosen to continue the journey? They did receive communication but distinguishing genuine finalists from impostors proved impossible. An interview with two alleged winners of the first puzzle revealed their experience on the dark web forum, where they communicated with established members of Cicada. According to their account, Cicada 3301 started as a small group with shared ideals about privacy and security but eventually expanded into an international organization.

The winners of the second puzzle shared a similar story, further emphasizing the idea that Cicada may be a group of privacy-conscious developers.

Cicada 3301's puzzles remain unsolved, and the group's motives and identity remain hidden. While the mystery continues, the most plausible theory suggests that Cicada is a loose-knit collective of privacy-minded hobby-cryptographers using complex puzzles to recruit talented individuals. As of April 2017, Cicada had left a final message urging vigilance against disinformation. The current status of the third puzzle and the possibility of a fourth puzzle are shrouded in secrecy, leaving Cicada 3301 as an enduring internet enigma.

21. Chasing D. B. Cooper: The Unsolved Heist

In the opening sequence, we are thrust into the audacious mid-air escape of an individual from a Boeing 727, situated somewhere over Reno. An immediate search of the aircraft ensued, but the identity, origin, and destination of this person remain shrouded in mystery. The pursuit continues, driven by the expectation of uncovering the truth.

On the afternoon of November 24, 1971, a man of middle age, carrying a briefcase, entered Portland International Airport and secured a one-way ticket to Seattle, Washington. This individual identified himself as Dan Cooper and, accompanied by 36 passengers and a crew of six, boarded Northwest Airlines Flight 305. Cooper, positioned in the rear-middle seats on the right side, proceeded to order a drink and, reflecting the norms of the 1970s, indulged in a cigarette. As the flight received clearance for departure, he handed an envelope to flight attendant Florence Schaffner, inside which was a handwritten note indicating the presence of a bomb. Schaffner reluctantly took her place beside him, catching sight of what appeared to be eight sticks of dynamite in his briefcase. Cooper's demands were clear: $200,000 in cash, four parachutes, and a fuel truck ready for the plane's refueling in Seattle. A threat of catastrophic action loomed if his demands were not met. Once the flight was airborne, Schaffner reported the situation to the cockpit crew, while another flight attendant named Tina Mucklow remained by Cooper's side, acting as an intermediary between him and the rest of the crew. For the next hour and a half, Flight 305 maintained a holding pattern near Seattle, as authorities at various levels rushed to secure the ransom and the parachutes. Ten thousand $20 bills were procured from a local bank, and the parachutes were supplied by the owner of a nearby skydiving school. The flight finally touched down in Seattle more than two hours past its scheduled time, under the cover of night. The ransom and parachutes were handed over to Mucklow in exchange for permitting passengers and two flight attendants to disembark. Cooper now requested to be flown to Mexico City, with specific flight parameters and equipment conditions. Two of his conditions could not be met initially. First, the specified flight configuration wouldn't allow for a non-stop flight to Mexico City, leading to a refueling stop in Reno, Nevada. Second, the ventral staircase could not be extended upon departure. Cooper consented to retract the stairs with the condition that Mucklow remained with him to teach him how to extend them in-flight. After a delay in Seattle due to refueling challenges, Flight 305 resumed its journey and Cooper instructed Mucklow to stay out of the cockpit and not disturb him. Shortly after takeoff, Cooper was last seen standing in the aisle, seemingly preparing to jump. Mucklow joined the rest of the crew in the cockpit, locked the door behind her, and, three hours later, Flight 305 safely landed in Reno. However, when the crew ventured to the rear of the cabin, they found no sign of Cooper or the bomb, except for a slightly damaged, extended aft stairway. It was apparent that, somewhere between Seattle and Reno, Cooper had donned a parachute, descended the stairs, and vanished into the dark night.

Chapter 2 - The Manhunt Begins:

The realization that Cooper was no longer on board prompted the swift arrival of numerous FBI agents, but they discovered only a limited amount of physical evidence, including a black clip-on tie, eight cigarette butts, and two of the four parachutes. Cooper seemed to have taken the ransom and the briefcase with him. Descriptions of Cooper from interviews conducted on the night of the hijacking characterized him as a middle-aged white man with brown eyes and dark hair, who wore a dark trench coat, a dark suit, a white shirt, a black tie, and dark shoes. He had also donned sunglasses after boarding. Based on this description, the FBI produced the first of several composite sketches. Determining when Cooper left the plane presented challenges, as no crew members or fighter jet pilots escorting the flight witnessed the jump due to the late hour. However, the crew noticed an oscillation or vibration of the aircraft roughly 10 minutes after the last communication with Cooper, suspecting it might be linked to his jump. This addressed the "when" aspect of the escape. As for the "where," Cooper had not specified a route, allowing the Captain to choose the flight path. They followed an airway known as Victor 23, estimating that the most likely location of Cooper's jump was about 40 kilometers north of Portland. The FBI commenced a vast search operation with helicopters, airplanes, and ground troops at dawn, but the expansive, rugged terrain and adverse weather complicated the effort.

Chapter 3 - Follow the Money:

By early December, the FBI shifted its focus to the $200,000 ransom, meticulously documented with serial numbers. This enabled authorities to share the serial numbers with various entities, making it challenging for Cooper to spend the money. Rewards were offered by Northwest Airlines and newspapers for anyone who found a note with a matching serial number. However, no such discoveries occurred until almost a decade later. In 1980, a young boy named Brian Ingram uncovered three bundles of cash totaling $5,880 while building a campfire on a beach in southern Washington. The money was found to match the ransom serial numbers, raising questions about how it ended up so far from the expected drop zone. Theories emerged, including the possibility of a different drop zone closer to the Washougal River. This find added complexity to the investigation.

Chapter 4 - A Leap of Faith:

From the outset, there was a prevailing belief that Cooper did not survive his audacious escape. While this outcome may lack the excitement of an alternative conclusion, it's crucial to acknowledge that reality often differs from the narrative. While there is no concrete evidence for or against Cooper's survival, the assumption that he met his demise holds merit.

When Cooper leaped into the darkness, Flight 305 was traversing a frigid rainstorm at an altitude of approximately 10,000 feet above southern Washington, traveling at roughly 170 knots. The fierce winds were strong enough to dislodge a placard from the aft stairway, which was later found in 1978 nearly directly beneath the estimated flight path. It's an understatement to say that Cooper was ill-prepared for this endeavor. Moreover, layers of clouds obscured the ground below, likely meaning that Cooper jumped without precise knowledge of his location. Even if he had visibility of the ground and a designated drop zone, the non-steerable parachute he used would have prevented him from directing his descent to a specific landing spot, making coordination with a ground-based accomplice unfeasible.

Though Cooper appeared to have some knowledge of parachutes, the mishap involving the dummy-chute and his selection of an older, technically inferior primary parachute may indicate less expertise than presumed. Nevertheless, these actions might have different explanations. For instance, the dummy-chute might have been used to secure the money, and Cooper's choice of the older military parachute could indicate familiarity, perhaps from military training. Notably, Cooper mentioned the proximity of McChord Air Force Base to Seattle-Tacoma Airport, possibly suggesting a military background.

Furthermore, Cooper's selection of a Boeing 727 for hijacking might be more than a random choice. This aircraft was utilized by the CIA for covert operations during the Vietnam War due to its unique aft stairway. Cooper's knowledge of this feature suggests he understood it provided a relatively safe means of escape. However, his choice of Northwest Airlines was apparently arbitrary, as he stated that Flight 305 was merely in the right place at the right time. While Cooper demonstrated considerable knowledge of aviation and the local terrain, he left minimal evidence, maintained a low profile to prevent panic, concealed his identity with sunglasses, and demanded four parachutes to deceive authorities into believing he was taking a hostage. He was also clever enough to retrieve the initial note he gave to Florence Schaffner. Yet, his lack of detailed planning for the escape route and destination change from Mexico City to Reno and the absence of essential parachuting gear raise questions about the meticulousness of his preparations.

On the other hand, no missing persons report matching Cooper's description emerged following the hijacking, suggesting the possibility of his survival and a quick, low-profile return to his normal life. Additionally, similar mid-air escapes by other hijackers led to their survival and subsequent apprehension. Despite the challenges of his escape, the absence of concrete evidence regarding Cooper's fate leaves open the intriguing possibility that he indeed survived.

Chapter 5 - The Suspects:

When the news of the hijacking reached the public, the FBI had already begun investigating several potential suspects. Among them was an individual in Portland with the initials D. B. and the surname Cooper. This particular Cooper was swiftly ruled out as a suspect. However, due to an error by the press, the name Dan Cooper was erroneously transposed to D. B. Cooper, and this misconception became a defining aspect of the case.

While it is highly likely that Dan Cooper used a pseudonym, there is a French comic book series bearing the same name. This series features a Canadian pilot named Dan Cooper. While the comic was not available in English or the United States before 1971, it was accessible in Canada, a country with a significant French-speaking population. Given that distinguishing American and Canadian accents can be challenging, there is a plausible theory that Cooper, described as having no distinct accent, may have been a bilingual Canadian. An interesting hint that supports this idea is the phrase "negotiable American currency" used by the Captain when relaying Cooper's demands to Air Traffic Control. The inclusion of "American currency" in the phrase could suggest that Cooper was not American. However, it's essential to note that there is uncertainty regarding whether this phrase directly originated from Cooper or if it was a paraphrase by the Captain. For instance, notes taken by the crew during the hijacking indicate the phrase "negotiable currency," while post-hijacking testimonies from the crew mention "$200,000 in cash" and "circulated US currency."

Therefore, there is a possibility that Cooper was Canadian and possibly took inspiration from the Dan Cooper comics for his alias. The precise details remain elusive, leaving room for speculation and intrigue.

Alternatively, just as he could have been American and might have derived his name from another source, it's worth acknowledging that there are multiple facets to this case. Almost fifty years have elapsed since the hijacking transpired, during which time, countless individuals have been probed and scrutinized as potential D. B. Cooper candidates. Naturally, it's unfeasible to delve into all these individuals here, but let's examine a few who, at various points, have aroused suspicion of being D. B. Cooper.

One of the earliest suspects, Robert Rackstraw, came under scrutiny in 1978, presenting a seemingly compelling case at first glance. He was a decorated Army paratrooper and a helicopter pilot with expertise in explosives. He also had an extensive criminal history and, intriguingly, an uncle named John Cooper, a skydiving enthusiast. Rackstraw's expulsion from the Army shortly before the hijacking might indicate a potential motive, given the hijacker's mentioned grudge. When questioned by journalists and private investigators, Rackstraw neither affirmed nor categorically denied being D. B. Cooper, often offering cryptic responses such as "I could have been" or "I would not discount myself." However, there were discrepancies, like his light-colored eyes, which didn't align with Cooper's description. Furthermore, Rackstraw's age of 28 at the time of the hijacking contradicted the mid-forties age range reported by most passengers and crew.

Kenneth Christiansen emerged as a suspect in 2003 when his brother noticed parallels between him and Cooper. Christiansen had briefly served as a paratrooper in World War II and had worked for Northwest Airlines as both a mechanic and a flight attendant since 1953. His age at the time of the hijacking, 45, matched the general description, and he was left-handed, potentially in line with Cooper. Intriguingly, Christiansen apparently left a mysterious statement shortly before his death in 1994: "There is something you should know, but I cannot tell you." After his passing, his family discovered over $200,000 in his bank accounts. To make matters more intriguing, Florence Schaffner, a flight attendant, mentioned that photographs of Christiansen bore a striking resemblance to Cooper. However, Christiansen fell short in terms of physical description, being shorter and lighter, and there were distinctions in hair, as noted in composite sketches. The large sums of money he accumulated were explained as proceeds from land sales.

Richard McCoy became a suspect in 1972 when he carried out a hijacking similar to D. B. Cooper's, using a Boeing 727 and escaping via the aft stairway. This shared modus operandi led some to believe the same person was responsible for both hijackings. McCoy used an alias, employed a phony hand-grenade to intimidate the crew, and issued handwritten demands, echoing several elements of the D. B. Cooper case. Both McCoy and Cooper employed the phrase "no funny stuff" as a warning to the crew and demanded $500,000 in cash and four parachutes. McCoy, however, bailed out over Utah, surviving his jump and evading authorities for two days before capture and a 45-year prison sentence. Before his death in 1974, McCoy refrained from confirming or denying his connection to D. B. Cooper. On the other hand, McCoy was an avid recreational skydiver, had skydiving equipment, gave precise flight path instructions, and used an unloaded handgun. He also failed to retrieve one of the notes he had handed to a flight attendant. McCoy's age, 29 at the time of the hijacking, diverged from the perceived mid-forties age of Cooper, and all three flight attendants confirmed that McCoy was not Cooper. While the cases shared several resemblances, it's plausible that McCoy was a copycat who had read about D. B. Cooper in the news.

Duane Weber came under suspicion in 1995 when, shortly before his death, he purportedly disclosed to his wife, "I've got a secret to tell you. I am Dan Cooper." Following his deathbed revelation, Weber's widow remembered numerous intriguing details, including finding a bank bag similar to the one used in the hijacking, claims of Weber sustaining a knee injury after parachuting from an aircraft, and a nightmare involving leaving fingerprints on the aft stairs. Weber, a World War II veteran, possessed an extensive criminal record and corresponded with the physical description. He was 47 years old in 1971. Nevertheless, Weber's fingerprints didn't match those collected from Flight 305, although it's uncertain if any of the prints genuinely belonged to Cooper. Additionally, his DNA didn't align with the DNA sample from the tie clasp. Regrettably, the evidence contained in eight cigarette butts, likely infused with Cooper's DNA, was lost and has yet to resurface.

William Smith emerged as a suspect in 2018. He had served in the Navy during World War II, likely gaining parachuting experience. At the time of the hijacking, he was 43, had dark brown eyes, and matched the general physical description. There was a likeness between Smith and composite sketches, particularly a speculative sketch of an older D. B. Cooper. A student named Ira Daniel Cooper, who had died in World War II, attended the same high school as Smith. Smith's professional background in a railroad company's yardmaster role was noteworthy. An electron microscope examination of the tie left behind by Cooper revealed various metallic particles, including rare pure titanium, potentially suggesting employment in a chemical or metallurgical facility or a rail yard. However, Smith had spent his life in the northeastern United States, far from the hijacking's location. This geographic discrepancy lessened his suitability as a suspect.

In conclusion, this limited selection of suspects serves to underscore the formidable challenges of definitively identifying D. B. Cooper in the absence of substantial evidence. Despite the striking dissimilarities among these five individuals, each one could potentially be D. B. Cooper. It remains unclear whether Cooper genuinely appeared.

22. Aztec Legacy: Unearthing an Ancient Civilization

Deep beneath the bustling streets of modern-day Mexico City lies the remnants of a once-mighty civilization, known as the Aztecs. Their tale is one of boundless power, unwavering ambition, and an indomitable connection to the divine. Initially, the Aztecs, also referred to as The Mex, were a nomadic tribe in Northern Mexico. According to legend, in the 13th century, they set out on a sacred journey guided by their deity, who provided a divine mission: to find a new homeland where they would witness an eagle perched on a cactus, devouring a snake. This sign led them to the swampy shores of Lake Texcoco, where they founded their grand city, Tenochtitlan, in the year 1325. This city was a marvel of engineering, featuring intricate canals, grand temples, and bustling markets. However, the path to establish this magnificent city was fraught with challenges. The Mexica, as they were known, faced hostility from neighboring tribes, limited resources, and the harsh realities of their new environment. Nevertheless, driven by determination, ingenuity, and an unshakable belief in their divine destiny, they transformed these challenges into opportunities.

Religion served as the cornerstone of Aztec society. The gods were believed to influence every facet of existence, from the changing seasons to the outcomes of battles. In gratitude, the Aztecs held grand ceremonies, offering gifts, dances, and, at times, human sacrifices to appease and honor their deities.

As we bid farewell to the first chapter of our exploration, we've only scratched the surface of the rich tapestry that is the Aztec civilization. Join us as we delve deeper into their world, examining their ascent to power, their daily lives, and the legacy they left behind.

From the marshy banks of Lake Texcoco, the Aztecs constructed not merely a city but an empire. Their rise to prominence was marked by strategic alliances, formidable military prowess, and an insatiable desire to expand. The Aztecs were fierce warriors, boasting a highly organized military with various ranks, specialized roles, and rigorous training. Warriors earned their status through acts of bravery in battle and the capture of enemies, a practice central to their religious rituals. However, the Aztecs were not solely warriors; they were also skilled diplomats. In 1428, under the leadership of Itscoatl, the Aztecs formed the Triple Alliance with the city-states of Texcoco and Tlacopan. This alliance laid the foundation for their dominance in the region, enabling them to embark on a series of conquests, subjugating neighboring city-states and expanding their territory. Tribute poured into Tenochtitlan, filling the city's coffers with goods, crops, and precious materials from across Mesoamerica. The wealth of the empire was evident in its capital; Tenochtitlan was a marvel of urban planning and architecture. At its center stood the Templo Mayor, a massive pyramid dedicated to the gods Tlaloc and Huitzilopochtli. This monumental structure was surrounded by plazas, palaces, and the homes of the nobility.

Yet, with great power came great responsibility. The Aztecs had a complex administrative system to govern their vast empire. Nobles, priests, and military leaders played crucial roles in governance, ensuring that tribute was collected, laws were upheld, and the gods were honored.

As the sun bathes the splendid city of Toosan in its golden light, we are reminded of the Aztecs' ingenuity, ambition, and resilience. Their meteoric rise to power was constructed upon a foundation of strategy, collaboration, and an unwavering faith in their destiny.

Beyond the grandeur of its temples and palaces, Tenochtitlan was a vibrant, living city, brimming with activity. Today, we embark on a journey to the heart of the Aztec capital, where we'll uncover the daily rhythms of life. This city was a marvel of urban planning, featuring a grid-like structure intersected by canals, which served as the primary means of transportation. Canoes laden with goods traversed these waterways, connecting neighborhoods and facilitating trade.

At the core of Tenochtitlan was the Tatalo marketplace, a bustling hub of commerce where traders from across Mesoamerica converged, offering a wide array of goods, from precious stones and exotic feathers to everyday items such as maize, beans, and textiles. Food held a central place in Aztec life, with maize, or corn, serving as the staple consumed in various forms like tortillas, tamales, and atole, a maize-based drink. The region's rich biodiversity provided an abundance of fruits, vegetables, and proteins.

Family and community formed the bedrock of Aztec society. Families lived in calpulli, large extended family groups that shared communal tasks and responsibilities. Children were imparted with values, traditions, and skills from a young age to ensure the continuity of their rich cultural heritage. Education was highly valued, with boys receiving training in warfare and civic duties while girls were taught household tasks and religious rituals. The elite attended the Cicak, an institution where they were groomed for leadership and the priesthood.

As the day drew to a close in Tenochtitlan, families gathered to share meals, stories, and dreams. The city, with its pulsating energy, showcased the Aztecs' ability to harmoniously blend the mundane with the divine, creating a vibrant tapestry of daily existence.

For the Aztecs, the cosmos was a vast and intricate tapestry interwoven with stories, deities, and mysteries. Tonight, we venture into the spiritual realm of the Aztecs to explore their deeply rooted beliefs and the gods that shaped their world.

The Aztec pantheon was vast and diverse, with gods representing natural forces, celestial bodies, and human emotions. At the pinnacle of this pantheon stood Quilille, the sun god, patron deity of Tenochtitlan, and embodiment of warfare and the sun. Tlaloc, the rain god, was revered for his life-giving rains and feared for his capacity to unleash storms and droughts, reflecting the Aztecs' understanding of the delicate balance of life.

Kukulkan, the Feathered Serpent, was a god of wind, learning, and culture, often depicted as a serpent adorned with feathers symbolizing the union of earth and sky. Goddess Cihuacoatl, portrayed with a skirt of serpents and a necklace of human hearts, represented the Earth's nurturing aspect as well as its capacity for destruction.

Religion permeated every facet of Aztec life, with rituals, ceremonies, and festivals held year-round to honor the gods and secure their favor. These ceremonies encompassed a range of activities, from dances and music to elaborate offerings and, at times, human sacrifices. The Aztecs believed that these sacrifices were essential to maintain cosmic balance and were conducted with deep reverence and precision, as the individuals chosen were seen as messengers to the gods.

Art played a fundamental role in Aztec life, serving as a medium for expression, communication, and devotion. Sculptors crafted intricate statues of gods, rulers, and mythical creatures from materials like stone and wood.

As the sun bathes the magnificent city of Toosan in its golden glow, we are prompted to reflect on the Aztecs' exceptional qualities of ingenuity, ambition, and unwavering resilience. Their rapid ascent to power was grounded in a bedrock of strategic planning, collaboration, and an enduring faith in their predetermined destiny.

Beyond the grandeur of the city's temples and palaces, Tenochtitlan thrived as a vibrant, living entity teeming with activity. Today, we embark on a journey to the heart of the Aztec capital, where we will uncover the daily cadence of life. The city was a feat of urban planning, designed with a grid-like layout intersected by canals, serving as the primary transportation routes. Canoes laden with goods traversed these waterways, connecting neighborhoods and facilitating trade.

At the center of Tenochtitlan lay the Tatalo marketplace, a bustling epicenter of commerce where traders from all corners of Mesoamerica converged, offering a rich array of goods, from precious stones to exotic feathers, symbolizing status and divine favor. Food held a central role in Aztec life, with maize, or corn, being the dietary staple, prepared in various forms such as tortillas, tamales, and atole, a maize-based beverage. The region's abundant biodiversity provided a wealth of fruits, vegetables, and protein sources.

Family and community formed the solid foundation of Aztec society, with families residing in calpulli, large extended family groups sharing communal tasks and responsibilities. Children were instilled with values, traditions, and skills from a young age to ensure the perpetuation of their rich cultural heritage. Education was highly valued, with boys receiving training in warfare and civic duties, while girls were instructed in household tasks and religious rituals. The elite attended the Cicak, an institution where they were groomed for leadership and the priesthood.

As the day drew to a close in Tenochtitlan, families gathered to share meals, stories, and dreams, showcasing the city's vibrant energy and the Aztecs' ability to harmoniously combine the mundane with the divine.

For the Aztecs, the cosmos represented a vast, intricate tapestry woven with stories, deities, and mysteries. Tonight, we embark on a journey into the spiritual realm of the Aztecs, delving into their deeply ingrained beliefs and the gods that shaped their world.

The Aztec pantheon was extensive and varied, with gods embodying natural forces, celestial bodies, and human emotions. At the zenith of this pantheon stood Quilille, the sun god, patron deity of Tenochtitlan and symbolizing warfare and the sun. Tlaloc, the rain god, was revered for his life-giving rains and feared for his capacity to bring storms and droughts, reflecting the Aztecs' understanding of the delicate balance of life.

Kukulkan, the Feathered Serpent, was a god of wind, learning, and culture, often depicted as a serpent adorned with feathers, symbolizing the union of the earth and sky. The goddess Cihuacoatl, portrayed with a skirt of serpents and a necklace of human hearts, symbolized the Earth's nurturing aspect and its potential for destruction.

Religion infused every facet of Aztec life, with rituals, ceremonies, and festivals held throughout the year to honor the gods and secure their favor. These ceremonies encompassed a range of activities, from dances and music to elaborate offerings and, at times, human sacrifices. The Aztecs believed these sacrifices were vital for maintaining cosmic balance, and they were performed with profound reverence and precision, as the individuals chosen were considered messengers to the gods.

Art played an integral role in Aztec life, serving as a medium for expression, communication, and devotion. Sculptors crafted intricate statues of gods, rulers, and mythical creatures from materials like stone and wood.

The Aztecs also excelled in crafting remarkable pieces using the vibrant feathers of native birds, a unique art form known as featherwork. These creations adorned the attire of nobles and priests, signifying their status and divine favor.

In the realm of science, the Aztecs exhibited a deep understanding of astronomy. They meticulously observed celestial bodies, leading to the creation of detailed calendars governing both religious ceremonies and agricultural cycles. The Aztecs were also skilled herbalists and physicians, utilizing a wide array of plants for medicinal purposes, treating various ailments and even performing surgeries with tools crafted from obsidian and bone.

Innovation thrived in the heart of Tenochtitlan, exemplified by the chinampas or floating gardens, a testament to Aztec ingenuity. These man-made islands, constructed on the shallow waters of Lake Texcoco, maximized agricultural output, ensuring the city's sustenance. The Aztecs also developed a complex system of writing using pictographs and glyphs, inscribed on materials made from bark paper or deer skin, to record history, rituals, and knowledge for future generations.

As we immerse ourselves in the world of Aztec art and innovation, we are reminded of their profound ability to harmoniously blend form and function, beauty and intellect. Their legacy is not confined to their conquests but is imprinted on the canvas of human achievement.

The Aztec empire, in all its grandeur, was not an isolated entity; it was an integral part of a vast Mesoamerican tapestry interwoven with numerous cultures and civilizations. While the Aztecs are often remembered for their military conquests, they were also astute diplomats. Alliances, marriages, and trade agreements played pivotal roles in their interactions with neighboring city-states. Trade was the lifeblood of Mesoamerica, and Tenochtitlan, with its strategic location, became a hub for merchants from distant lands. Cacao from the south, turquoise from the north, and obsidian from nearby regions flowed into the city's markets. The Aztecs maintained a delicate balance with their tributary states, where they received tribute while providing protection and stability in return. Cultural exchanges were also prevalent, as the Aztecs adopted and adapted various practices, art forms, and technologies from their neighbors. This fusion enriched their society, making it a melting pot of Mesoamerican traditions.

However, relations were not always harmonious, as rivalries, territorial disputes, and differences in beliefs occasionally led to conflicts. Yet even in warfare, the Aztecs often sought to integrate conquered peoples, recognizing the strength in diversity. It is through connections, exchanges, and sometimes conflicts that cultures evolve, adapt, and leave lasting legacies.

Every civilization, no matter how grand, faces moments of reckoning. For the Aztecs, the zenith of their power was met with challenges from within and beyond their borders. While the Aztec empire expanded and flourished, it was not without internal pressures. The demands of tribute and human sacrifice strained relations with subjugated city-states, leading to pockets of rebellion and dissent. Nature, too, posed challenges, as droughts and famines tested the Aztecs' agricultural ingenuity and their relationship with the gods. Even the very canals and chinampas that once symbolized their mastery over nature became strained as resources dwindled.

Yet the most formidable challenge would come from across the seas. In 1519, Spanish conquistadors, led by Hernan Cortez, arrived on the shores of Mesoamerica. Initially received as guests, the relationship between the Aztecs and the Spanish quickly soured due to

misunderstandings and the Spaniards' insatiable desire for gold. Tensions escalated, and the Spaniards, armed with advanced weaponry and horses, proved formidable. However, it was not just steel and gunpowder that they brought with them; diseases unknown to the Aztecs decimated the population, weakening the once-mighty empire. The culmination of these challenges led to the siege of

Tenochtitlan in 1521. After months of fierce fighting, the city fell, marking the end of the Aztec empire.

The sun set on Tenochtitlan, but its legacy was not extinguished. The fusion of Aztec and Spanish cultures gave birth to a new era, shaping the destiny of a nation and leaving an indelible mark on the annals of history. As our journey through the annals of the Aztec civilization draws to a close, we are left with a mosaic of memories, achievements, and lessons that transcend time. The Aztecs, with their complexities and contradictions, remind us of the timeless dance between humanity and nature, between the known and the mysterious. As we step into the future, their legacy serves as a beacon, illuminating the path of understanding, respect, and unity.

23. The Enigma of Indus Valley: Uncovering Untold Secrets

In 1827, a soldier in the service of the British East India Company, James Lewis, became disillusioned with the company's activities and chose to desert the army. In order to go incognito, he assumed a new identity and pursued his passion, which was traveling. After journeying across the Indian subcontinent for two years, he arrived in the Punjab region in 1829, where he stumbled upon the ruins of an ancient city. At that time, he had no knowledge of the age of these ruins or the civilization to which they belonged. However, due to his deep interest in history, he began to meticulously document everything he encountered, including notes and drawings, some of which are still attributed to James Lewis.

Remarkably, James Lewis was unaware that he had stumbled upon the ancient city of Harappa. It was only a century later, in the 1920s, that more information about this ancient civilization began to surface. John Marshall was appointed as the director of the Archaeological Survey of India (ASI), and with the assistance of Indian archaeologists, he conducted a comprehensive survey of the Harappa ruins. It was determined that these ruins were over 5,000 years old. Simultaneously, another historical site was discovered on the banks of the Indus River, which was named Mohenjo-Daro, meaning the "Mound of the Dead." Further excavations unveiled additional such ruins, leading to the realization that these buried sites held evidence of a previously unknown civilization. Due to their proximity to the Indus River, this civilization was named the Indus Valley Civilization.

As of 2022, we have acquired substantial knowledge about this civilization, which is now part of school curricula. Yet, two mysteries continue to confound us: the first pertains to the Harappan language, their script, and its decipherment. The second revolves around the demise of this remarkable civilization. What led to the decline and disappearance of these people?

The Indus Valley Civilization, a Bronze Age civilization, was located in the regions that are now Pakistan, Afghanistan, and Northwest India. Over 1,400 sites have been discovered to date, with 900 of them situated in India. It coexisted with only a few other civilizations during its time, including the Egyptian, Mesopotamian, and Chinese civilizations. Of these, the Chinese civilization was the most recent, while the Indus Valley, Egyptian, and Mesopotamian civilizations are considered to be the oldest. While Mesopotamia is traditionally believed to be the oldest civilization, a study conducted by IIT Kharagpur and the ASI in 2016 using archaeological dating techniques suggested that the Indus Valley Civilization might be as old as 8,000 years. Evidence of farming settlements dating back to 7,000 BC has been discovered, mainly in present-day Haryana. The period from 7,000 BC to 5,500 BC is referred to as the Pre-Harappan Phase, during which cities had yet to develop, and agricultural tools and pottery were prevalent. Urbanization is believed to have begun around 5,500 BC, marked by the establishment of public buildings and trade routes. By 2,600 BC, the civilization had advanced to the point of constructing multi-story brick houses in its cities, using standardized bricks of identical dimensions. Each house was equipped with a toilet, bathing area, and a drainage system for water and waste disposal, along with well-planned road gutters, footpath trees, public wells, and dustbins. Their urban planning was remarkably advanced, rivaling modern Indian cities in terms of infrastructure.

However, the greatest challenge in understanding this civilization is the decipherment of the Harappan script, known as the Indus Script. Over 4,000 artifacts containing inscriptions have been found, and numerous attempts have been made to decode them since the 1920s. Despite these efforts, the meaning of these symbols remains elusive. Some insights have been gleaned from the script; for instance, it is believed to have been written from right to left, unlike languages written from left to right. Additionally, it was observed that inscriptions often featured a block of text at the top in the Indus Script followed by a large animal symbol underneath. The most common animal depicted in these inscriptions resembled a unicorn, a creature that may not have existed in reality.

The Indus Valley Civilization was a remarkable chapter in human history, offering an advanced urban society with sophisticated infrastructure, yet its language and script remain a tantalizing mystery, as does the ultimate cause of its decline.

The reason behind the consistent presence of animal depictions alongside their writings is a perplexing question. Additionally, these images might appear to require extensive surfaces, but, in reality, these stone seals are relatively small, measuring approximately 2.5 cm² to 5 cm² in size. Hence, the engravings were not on large surfaces. Furthermore, historians meticulously examined and cataloged the signs and symbols of the Indus Script, discovering the existence of more than 400 distinct signs within their script. To put this into perspective, while the English language consists of 26 alphabets, the Indus Script boasted over 400 unique symbols. Although some of these symbols resemble stick figures, various creatures such as fish, turtles, crabs, insects, and birds are discernible. Due to the sheer abundance of symbols in this script, historians posit that it is, in fact, a Logosyllabic Script, which means it utilizes symbols to represent words or sounds. To illustrate, consider the Egyptian hieroglyphs, a script from the Egyptian civilization. Remarkably, historians have successfully decoded this language, understanding the meaning of each symbol within the Egyptian script. In this script, each symbol represents a specific sound. For instance, the symbol of a vulture signifies the sound '/aa,' and the symbol of a leg represents the sound '/b.' Each sound is similarly associated with its respective symbol. Thus, we can comprehend the meaning of each sound in the Egyptian hieroglyphs, a feat made possible by the discovery of the Rosetta Stone, an ancient artifact with inscriptions in both Egyptian hieroglyphs and ancient Greek. Unfortunately, no such "Rosetta Stone" or comparable tablet has been found to assist in deciphering the Indus Script. Consequently, the Indus language remains enigmatic and inaccessible. It is an incredibly daunting task to deduce the meanings of these words and symbols. To elucidate, imagine being given a piece of Chinese literature without access to any Chinese translation, unaware of the existence of the Chinese language. Attempting to decipher the Chinese symbols in such a scenario would be an exceedingly formidable challenge. Nonetheless, historians have discerned certain patterns within the Indus language. For instance, in the English language, we can effortlessly generate a list of words commencing with 'W,' such as Weather, Wire, Water, and Watermelon. However, when prompted to produce words commencing with 'WZ' or 'WQ,' our options are limited, as no such English words exist. This illustrates the presence of patterns within languages; for instance, the English language has 26 alphabets, and these alphabets form specific combinations that adhere to discernible patterns. In the Indus Script, certain symbols consistently follow others, indicating a structured pattern. For instance, whenever a diamond-shaped symbol is employed, it is invariably succeeded by the symbol of two parallel lines, but it is never succeeded by the symbol of a stick figure. Moreover, the most frequently used symbol resembles a jar and is frequently encountered at the conclusion of the Indus script text, possibly signifying the end of a sentence. An intriguing revelation occurred when the Indus Script was discovered in Mesopotamia, which encompasses present-day Iraq and Iran. Notably, these regions featured different languages, as confirmed by the presence of diverse scripts. The most fascinating observation was that the pattern in the Indus script, with the jar-shaped symbol at the end of the text, was distinct from the script found in Mesopotamia, where the jar-shaped symbol was repeated twice. Surprisingly, the Indus Valley sites did not feature this double repetition of the jar-shaped symbol. This mystery raises the possibility that the people residing in Mesopotamia may have been using the Indus script to transcribe their own language. To clarify this concept further, consider that Hindi is written in the Devanagari script, featuring characters like क, ख, ग, घ. In contrast, English is written in the Latin script, incorporating letters such as A, B, C, D. Interestingly, German, French, and several other languages also use the Latin script, with shared alphabets like A, B, C, D. However, the spoken language may not necessarily align with the script used for writing. Although there is often a correlation between spoken language and script, the two can diverge. For example, imagine writing Hindi in the Latin script, a practice that is now commonplace.

"What are you currently engaged in? If we were to transliterate this Hindi phrase into the Latin script of English, we would spell 'क्या' as 'KYA.' This practice essentially entails writing Hindi using the Latin script, though the underlying language remains Hindi. Historians propose a parallel approach for the Mesopotamians concerning the Indus script, suggesting that they inscribed their language using this script. Consequently, distinctive patterns emerged in Mesopotamian inscriptions that differed from those in the Indus Valley. Consider the Hindi phrase 'आराम कर रहा हूँ' (I am resting). When transliterated into Latin, 'आराम' becomes 'AARAM,' with two 'A's at the beginning. Such a double 'A' initiation does not align with the conventions of the English language, wherein words do not commence with double 'A.' This illustrates how the script's pattern was modified.

Transitioning from language to the urban layout of the Indus Valley Civilization, a striking pattern emerges across the excavated cities. In all discovered cities of the Indus Valley Civilization, a common structural design is evident. Each city exhibits two main segments: a 'Lower Mount' enclosed by boundary walls from all sides and an

'Upper Mount' citadel built on elevated terrain, typically located to the west of the city. Both the citadel and the lower region possess their respective boundary walls. The citadel encompassed crucial public spaces such as marketplaces and workshops, serving as communal gathering areas. The construction of these walls primarily aimed to repel wild animals and safeguard the cities against floods, rather than protect against human threats, as the absence of natural enemies or invasions is indicated.

An insightful portrayal of the city structure of Mohenjo-Daro can be found in the film bearing the same name, featuring Hrithik Roshan. The film offers a relatively accurate representation of the city. A prominent attraction in Mohenjo-Daro is the Great Bath, a substantial multistoried bathing pool measuring 900 square feet in area with a depth of 2.4 meters. Constructed from fired bricks and waterproofed using natural tar, the bath featured a drainage hole and a well, ensuring a constant supply of fresh water. The maintenance of cleanliness in Mohenjo-Daro, in conjunction with the advanced drainage systems, suggests that this city possibly served as the capital of the Indus Valley Civilization.

Distinguishing the Indus Valley Civilization from Mesopotamia and Egypt is the absence of temples, mosques, religious sites, palaces, royal tombs, monarchs, priests, religious leaders, and military evidence within the former. This notable distinction from other Bronze Age civilizations highlights the societal uniqueness of the Harappan Civilization, marked by contentment, peaceful coexistence, and the absence of social hierarchies. This topic remains a subject of spirited debate, with differing views among historians.

Another significant unresolved mystery pertains to the decline of the Indus Valley Civilization. Archaeological records indicate a rapid decline between 1900 BC and 1300 BC, characterized by the cessation of city planning, neglect of sewer and drainage systems, the accumulation of waste in the Great Bath, and the discontinuation of trade with Mesopotamia. By 1800 BC, most cities lay abandoned, and the uniformity of writing systems, standardized weights, and building ratios disappeared. The exact cause of this decline remains unknown, giving rise to several theories.

One theory posits that the river on which the civilization depended, possibly the Saraswati River, began to dry up due to geological shifts or natural course alterations, prompting the inhabitants to migrate eastward to the Ganga River.

The second theory attributes deforestation to the civilization's downfall. This theory suggests that excessive deforestation, driven by the need for bricks and cattle fodder, eradicated the region's greenery, rendering it uninhabitable.

The third theory posits that a devastating disease may have swept through the population, similar to malaria or cholera, which were prevalent at the time.

While these theories offer plausible explanations, the exact cause of the Indus Valley Civilization's decline remains elusive. What is clear is that after 600 BC, this civilization had ceased to exist. The civilization, which endured for thousands of years—more than 5,000 years—met an unfortunate end. It is a testament to the impermanence of civilizations and how these settlements, once thriving, were buried over time, replaced by new cities and civilizations. This cycle persisted for thousands of years until James Lewis rediscovered the Indus Valley Civilization.

24. In the Shadow of Jack the Ripper: The Murders Unveiled

Jack the Ripper, a serial killer whose identity remains unknown, claimed five canonical victims in 1888 in London's East End. In that year, Victorian England found London's East End, specifically Whitechapel, to be a densely populated and squalid slum inhabited by nearly a million of the city's most impoverished residents. The streets reeked of filth, and living conditions were abysmal. Alcohol addiction was prevalent, offering solace at the bottom of gin bottles. Many women resorted to prostitution as a means of surviving their dire poverty.

One of these women was Marianne "Polly" Nichols, a 44-year-old. Nichols, struggling with alcoholism, had been unable to maintain her employment as a domestic servant in London. After losing her job, she sought refuge in a common lodging house. On the night of August 30, 1888, Nichols was struggling to pay for her bed. To raise funds, she left the lodging house around 11 pm with the intention of prostituting herself. Her former roommate, Ellen Holland, tried to convince her to return, given that it was nearing 2 am. Nichols, however, claimed to have raised her lodging money three times already that night but had spent it all on alcohol. She seemed unconcerned, and the two parted ways. Nichols was last seen walking toward Whitechapel Road.

Approximately one hour later, her lifeless body was discovered. The death of a prostitute was not uncommon in Whitechapel, given the dangerous nature of the profession. However, Nichols' murder was particularly shocking. Her throat bore deep cuts from two wounds, one of which had severed the tissue down to the vertebrae. Violent incisions marred her abdomen on both sides, with a deep, jagged wound partly ripping open the lower portion of her abdomen, causing her bowels to protrude. Nichols had not just been killed; she had been gruesomely mutilated.

A week later, on September 8, 1888, the body of 47-year-old Annie Chapman was found. Similar to Nichols, Chapman battled alcoholism, lived in a lodging house, and turned to prostitution for income. Chapman's throat, like Nichols, had been slashed, severing her vocal cord, rendering her unable to scream. Her abdomen was completely sliced open, and she had been disemboweled. Sections of flesh from her stomach were deliberately placed on her shoulders, while her small intestines had been removed and arranged above her right shoulder. The autopsy revealed that parts of her bladder were also taken, likely as macabre keepsakes.

In the early morning hours of September 30, 1888, the killer struck again, claiming two victims in close succession. The first was Elizabeth Stride, 44 years old, found by Louis Diemshutz, the steward of the International Working Men's Education Club. Stride's body was discovered in a poorly lit yard, without the mutilations inflicted on the previous victims. Her throat bore a single knife wound, and her body remained warm, suggesting that her death occurred shortly before its discovery.

Not satisfied with Stride's death, the killer targeted Catherine Eddowes, 46 years old, found about a mile away from Stride's body in Mitre Square. Eddowes had been drinking heavily on the night of her murder. Her throat was severed, like the other victims, and she was disemboweled, with intestines placed over her right shoulder. This time, the killer went further with mutilation, disfiguring her face. Her nose was removed, her cheeks were slashed, and vertical cuts were incised through each eyelid. The police surgeon believed that these mutilations were At least five minutes would have been necessary to complete this gruesome act. Two weeks later, on the 16th of October, the Whitechapel Vigilance Committee received a male parcel containing a human kidney, along with a letter claiming it was from Eddowes's body. Many contemporary observers and most modern historians, however, believe that the kidney was not authentic and more likely sent as a prank.

The murders of Stride and Eddowes eventually became known as the "double event." This time, a clue was left near the crime scene in Gulston Street, just a short walk from Mitre Square. Police discovered a section of Eddowes's bloodied apron, with a chalk inscription on the wall directly above it that read: "The Jews are the men that will not be blamed for nothing." The message seemed to suggest that Jewish individuals or the Jewish people were responsible for the series of murders. It remains unclear whether this statement was written by the murderer who intentionally placed the apron or if it was merely incidental and unrelated to the case, as graffiti was common in Whitechapel. Police Commissioner Charles Warren was concerned that the graffiti might incite anti-Semitic riots and ordered it to be washed away before dawn.

Mary Jane Kelly was the final known victim of Jack the Ripper. Unlike the other victims, Kelly was considerably younger at just 25 years old. She was murdered on Friday, the 9th of November 1888. Similar to the other four victims, Kelly had been living as a prostitute.

In contrast to the other victims who were murdered outdoors and had their mutilations performed hastily, Kelly was killed in the small room she rented at 13 Miller's Court off Dorset Street. This afforded her killer an extended period to take their time in disfiguring and mutilating her body. On the night she was murdered, she was last seen alive by a witness named George Hutchinson. They met around 2 a.m. on Commercial Street, where she asked him for a loan of sixpence. When he didn't have it, she walked in the direction of Thrall Street. Along the way, she was picked up by a well-dressed man who accompanied her to her lodgings on Dorset Street. Hutchinson described the man in Kelly's company as wearing a coat trimmed with astrakhan fur, a black tie with a horseshoe pin, button-over boots, and a large gold chain hanging from his waistcoat. Police questioned the credibility of Hutchinson's description, fueling debates regarding the Ripper's social class.

The shocking discovery of Kelly's mutilated body was made the next morning. Her landlord, John McCarthy, sent his assistant, former soldier Thomas Boyer, to collect the rent, as Kelly was six weeks behind in payments, owing 29 shillings. Boyer knocked on her door, received no response, and moved aside some clothing that had been used to plug a broken window. Peering through the window, he found Kelly's extensively mutilated corpse lying on the bed. Kelly's body was in the middle of the bed, with her shoulders flat but slightly inclined to the left, and her head turned on its left side.

Her throat had been severed down to the spine, and her face was hacked beyond recognition, with her nose, cheeks, eyebrows, and ears partially removed. Her abdomen had been almost entirely emptied of its organs, and both breasts were sliced off. Her uterus, kidneys, and one breast had been placed beneath her head, while the other breast was on her right foot. Her liver was found between her feet, and the spleen was located on the left side of her body. Her intestines had been removed and scattered around her feet, with sections draped upon the bedside table. Her thighs had been stripped of skin, flesh, and muscle, while her heart was missing from the crime scene, leading to speculation that the killer took it with them. The murderer is estimated to have spent about two hours with her body. Dr. Thomas Bond and Dr. Baxter Phillips, who examined the body, believed that Kelly had died between three to nine hours before being discovered. Phillips thought that, like the other victims, Kelly's life had been ended by the slash to her throat and the subsequent mutilations. Bond stated in his report that the knife used was about one inch wide and at least eight inches long, indicating that the murderer lacked specialized medical training or knowledge. However, it was clear that the killer needed to perform not only the murders but also the mutilations as part of a macabre ritual.

While some researchers may disagree, Mary Kelly is generally regarded as the Ripper's final victim. It is often assumed that the crimes ceased because the culprit either died, was imprisoned, institutionalized, or emigrated out of the city. The Jack the Ripper murders posed a significant challenge for Victorian police, who had little experience in handling such crimes. Detectives were searching for a killer who left very few clues. The police lacked many of the techniques and tools available to modern investigators, including fingerprinting, modern forensics, and psychological profiling. Crime scene photography, commonly used today, was not employed during that era.

The murders took place in one of London's most crime-ridden neighborhoods, where the clandestine nature of criminal elements and the general mistrust of the police by Whitechapel residents posed significant challenges for the investigation. During and after the murders, the police department and local press received hundreds of letters claiming to be authored by the murderer. Most of these letters were promptly dismissed as fakes, attributed to individuals seeking to generate fear or even to journalists aiming to boost newspaper sales. Ripper experts have largely disregarded nearly all of these letters as hoaxes. However, there is a possibility that at least one of the letters might have been a genuine clue from the killer.

On October 16, 1888, George Lusk, the President of the Whitechapel Vigilance Committee, received a three-inch square cardboard box in the mail. Inside the box was a letter, disturbingly containing half of a human kidney preserved in wine. The letter, which included spelling errors, read as follows:

"George Lutsk

From Hell

Mr. Lusk, Sir, I send you half the kidney I took from one woman and preserved it for you. Tell her peace, I fried and ate it; it was very nice. I may send you the bloody knife that took it out if you wait a while longer.

Signed, Catch me when you can, Mr. Lusk."

Regarding Emma Smith, initially, there was suspicion that the murders might be linked to local criminal gangs in the area, as prostitutes were often under the control of such gangs. It was believed that the victims had been attacked by their pimps as punishment or as a means of intimidating and warning other women under their control. Emma Smith was murdered by one such gang in Whitechapel on April 4, 1888. She was bludgeoned and attacked by at least two or three men, but she initially survived this assault and reported the attack. Some have considered her a possible Ripper victim, but this seems unlikely.

By early September 1888, the police abandoned the idea that the murders were gang-related. They concluded that the publicity surrounding the murders would have likely led to a member of the gang informing on the others. Consequently, the police shifted their focus to looking for a lone assassin.

John Piser, also known as "Leather Apron" due to the leather apron he wore for work, was a Polish Jew in Whitechapel. Locals reported that he ran an extortion racket, threatened prostitutes, and was always seen carrying a knife. Although he initially fit the profile of the killer, he had alibis for the nights of the two most recent murders and was ruled out as a suspect.

Severan Klosowski, known as George Chapman, was another suspect. He worked as a barber in Whitechapel and was investigated by Chief Inspector Frederick Aberline. Chapman was known to go out at night for extended periods, but there was little evidence linking him to the crimes at the time. He later poisoned three of his wives using tartar emedic, a compound resulting in a painful death similar to arsenic poisoning. Despite his guilt in those poisonings, most experts do not consider Chapman a likely Ripper suspect due to differences in the killings.

Francis Tumblety, an Irish-American, posed as an Indian herb doctor and resided in Whitechapel during the time of the murders. He was known for his extreme hatred of women, particularly prostitutes, and collected preserved female reproductive organs. Tumblety was arrested in 1888 for alleged homosexuality, a criminal offense at the time, but he fled to New York just before the murder of Mary Kelly. Although there were suspicions, he was never extradited to England, and to this day, Tumblety remains a possible suspect.

Aaron Kosminski, a Polish Jew who emigrated to England, was a hairdresser in Whitechapel during the time of the murders. He was regarded as insane, experiencing auditory hallucinations, paranoia, and poor hygiene. Police considered him a prime suspect during the initial investigation. In 2014, a shawl belonging to Catherine Eddowes, the Ripper's fourth victim, was found, and DNA analysis suggested a link to Kosminski's relatives. However, the findings have been met with skepticism, as the shawl might have been contaminated over the years. While doubts persist, it remains the strongest piece of forensic evidence connecting a suspect to the crimes.

Over a century later, the Jack the Ripper murders continue to be one of history's most famous and enduring mysteries, inspiring a vast industry of books, films, TV shows, and graphic novels. The murder sites have become a macabre tourist attraction, drawing tourists who seek to retrace Jack the Ripper's steps and the unfortunate paths of his victims.

25. The Loch Ness Enigma: Decoding the Monster Mystery

In the annals of mysterious creatures, the Loch Ness Monster, affectionately known as Nessie, holds a special place. Its legend has captivated the world's imagination for nearly a century, and the story began in earnest with the emergence of the infamous "surgeon's photo" in 1934. The image depicted a mysterious creature rising from the depths of Loch Ness, setting off a frenzy of public interest and an influx of tourists eager to catch a glimpse of the elusive beast. But even from the outset, questions about the photo's authenticity were raised.

Dr. R. Kenneth Wilson, the man who submitted the photo to the Daily Mail, fervently claimed it was genuine. However, skeptics argued that what appeared to be Nessie's neck and head was, in fact, something entirely different. The most prevalent theory suggested it was an elephant's trunk emerging from the water or perhaps a dolphin's fin. What's more, the photo published was substantially cropped and zoomed in, muddling the creature's shape and distorting any sense of scale or perspective.

Intriguingly, when experts later examined the original, uncropped photo, they saw something entirely different. The creature in question, they contended, was nowhere near the reported 20 feet in length. Instead, it seemed to measure a mere three feet at most. Could the most iconic photo of Nessie be a forgery?

In 1994, the photograph's authenticity came into question when a deathbed confession by Christian Sperling, stepson of a big-game hunter and filmmaker named Marmaduke Duke Weatherall, shed new light on the matter. Sperling revealed that in 1933, Weatherall had been hired by the Daily Mail to find evidence of the Loch Ness

Monster. He claimed that Weatherall had faked the photo, which set in motion a series of deceptions to save his reputation.

Weatherall turned to his stepson, a model maker, and together they created a model of a creature with a long neck and a small head, using plastic wood and a toy submarine. Weatherall then went to the Loch with his son and took the now-infamous photograph, which was, in reality, a picture of the model floating in the water.

The surgeon's photo became a game-changer, inciting a torrent of tourism that continues to this day. Yet, it was far from the last chapter in the Nessie mystery.

Over the years, there have been numerous other alleged sightings and photos of the Loch Ness Monster, but all have eventually been debunked. Nevertheless, the legend persisted, fueled by the human desire for attention and the thrill of the unknown.

In 2016, researchers from Kongsberg Maritime sent an underwater drone deep into Loch Ness, hoping to find definitive evidence of the creature. To their surprise, the sonar returned images resembling the head and neck of the supposed monster. Excitement surged until it was revealed that the object was a movie prop used in the 1969 Sherlock Holmes film shot in the Loch. Director Billy Wilder had removed humps from the prop, inadvertently causing it to sink to the bottom.

While the history of Nessie is fraught with deception and hoaxes, there are some intriguing pieces of evidence that keep the legend alive. In 1808, on the Scottish island of Stronsay, just 120 miles from Loch Ness, a strange creature's rotting carcass washed up on the beach. Eyewitnesses described a creature with a serpentine-like body, a long neck, and six limbs resembling paws. They called it the Stronsay Beast, and its physical description bears a striking resemblance to the Loch Ness Monster.

These accounts of a creature found near Loch Ness almost two centuries ago raise the possibility that the Loch Ness Monster could indeed be a real, undiscovered species. The proximity of Stronsay to Loch Ness, coupled with the creature's description, fuels the belief that Nessie could be a distant relative or even a younger specimen of the Stronsay Beast.

The Loch Ness Monster continues to elude definitive proof, and as technology advances, so does our capacity to investigate its existence. In a world filled with hoaxes and deception, Nessie remains one of the most enduring and captivating mysteries, reminding us that there is still much we don't understand about our world. And the possibility that a true discovery may yet await in the depths of Loch Ness keeps the legend alive for those who dare to believe.

26. Stonehenge's Builders: Did Aliens Lend a Hand?

Salisbury Plain, England - 2021: Stonehenge, the enigmatic circle of giant stones that has drawn millions of visitors over the years, continues to baffle and captivate researchers and tourists alike. Among those who have ventured to this iconic landmark is Michael Goff, a UK-based researcher. His visit in 2021 sparked a fascinating new theory about the purpose of Stonehenge, and it's a theory that revolves around time.

Stonehenge has always been a source of wonder and intrigue. Its massive stones, some weighing up to 45 tons, stand in a formation that has left people pondering for centuries how these ancient builders accomplished such an impressive feat. The questions are not just about the "why" but also the "how." How were these colossal stones transported to the site from distant locations, and how were they precisely positioned to create this remarkable monument?

Goff's theory delves into the latter question, attempting to unlock the mysteries of how Stonehenge could have been used as a timekeeping device. While Stonehenge is known for its alignment with the heavens and the changing seasons, Goff's theory suggests it served an even more precise timekeeping function.

According to Goff, to understand the clock-like mechanism of Stonehenge, we must reimagine the way we measure time. Our conventional 24-hour day, he argues, does not align with the monument's design. Instead, Stonehenge's intricate arrangement might be better suited for a 30-hour day. In such a system, each hour would be approximately 48 minutes long.

Goff's theory is rooted in the observation that the ancient Stonehenge site may have had moving parts that have since been lost. These moving parts, which could have been small stones or pieces of wood, allowed the monument to track the time of day as well as the time of the year. To recalibrate the timekeeping mechanism, the Stonehenge builders could have used a particular constellation, the Southern Cross, which would have been visible on the horizon during the monument's construction.

One of the intriguing elements of this theory is the requirement for Stonehenge to be transported from its original location at Wales to its current site. Goff's theory posits that the builders moved Stonehenge to keep it aligned with the Southern Cross as the Earth's tilt shifted over the centuries.

Goff's idea seems revolutionary, as it introduces a unique perspective on the purpose and function of Stonehenge. While it remains speculative and is yet to gain consensus among scholars, it is a testament to the enduring mystery of Stonehenge and the lengths people are willing to go to unlock its secrets.

Critics and skeptics may argue that Goff's theory has yet to be definitively proven, and it may remain one of many competing hypotheses about the purpose of Stonehenge. Nevertheless, it serves as a reminder of the enigma that Stonehenge continues to be, a testament to ancient human ingenuity, and the capacity of human curiosity to unlock the mysteries of our past.

The timeless allure of Stonehenge, with its ancient stones and secrets, continues to cast its spell over researchers and visitors alike. Despite the passage of millennia, it remains a symbol of human fascination with the unknown and the enduring quest to unravel the mysteries of our history.

27. Noah's Ark Quest: In Search of the Real Ark

Turkey - 1959: Army Captain Ilhan Durupanar, on a routine aerial reconnaissance mission for NATO, took a photograph that would become central to one of the most enduring biblical mysteries in history. Flying over the remote Turkish Highlands, Durupanar noticed a peculiar formation among the rocks below. Little did he know that this chance discovery would lead to the revival of an age-old legend: the mystery of Noah's Ark.

The story of Noah's Ark is an ancient tale told in the biblical Book of Genesis. In this narrative, humanity becomes increasingly sinful and corrupt, prompting God to unleash a cataclysmic flood that would wipe out all life on Earth, except for the righteous Noah and the animals he took on his ark. After 40 days and 40 nights of torrential rain, the ark comes to rest on the Mountains of Ararat.

Over the centuries, scholars and historians have debated whether the story of the great flood was a metaphor or a historical account. Could Noah's Ark be a real vessel, and if so, where did it come to rest? These questions remained unanswered until a series of discoveries and theories began to shed new light on the ancient tale.

In 1959, Captain Durupanar's aerial photograph captured what appeared to be the remains of a large ship, far inland and situated 6,500 feet above sea level. The anomaly sparked intrigue and renewed the quest to locate Noah's Ark. But it wasn't until later revelations that the mystery deepened.

In 1985, a British Air Force veteran, Leonard Simmons, discovered a 4,000-year-old clay tablet in his attic. Covered in cuneiform script, this tablet contained an account of a devastating flood event. Dr.

Irving Finkel, the Chief Curator for Near Eastern Artifacts at the British Museum, realized the significance of the tablet and sought to translate it. The text provided an account that closely paralleled the story of Noah's Ark, as found in the Bible.

But this discovery was not the only piece of the puzzle. In the late 1990s, a team of geologists, geophysicists, and oceanographers led by Americans William Ryan and Walter Pittman uncovered evidence of a massive Black Sea Deluge that dated back thousands of years. This deluge was theorized to have resulted from the sudden collapse of a glacier, causing a surge of seawater into the Black Sea region. The catastrophic flood event could have affected thousands of people, providing a basis for the flood narratives passed down through generations.

Furthermore, the ancient Mesopotamian Epic of Gilgamesh, dating back to 3,000 to 4,000 years ago, bore remarkable similarities to the story of Noah's Ark. The epic recounts a great flood sent by the gods, and a hero named Utnapishtim, who constructs an ark to save humanity and animals. This story, which predates the biblical account of Noah, raises questions about the origin and the universality of the flood narrative.

The mystery of Noah's Ark continues to captivate researchers and scholars worldwide, as they explore the connections between ancient texts, geological evidence, and chance discoveries. While these findings have not definitively proven the existence of Noah's Ark, they have reignited the debate and offered new insights into the ancient story of survival in the face of a catastrophic flood.

The story of Noah's Ark remains a testament to the enduring power of ancient legends, the curiosity of researchers, and the age-old quest to uncover the truths hidden in the sands of time. The hunt for the ark continues, driven by the desire to unravel one of humanity's most enduring mysteries.

28. The Dyatlov Pass Incident: Mountain of Secrets

"In the early months of 1959, a group of hikers embarked on a challenging expedition through the mountainous region of western Soviet Union. Comprising nine experienced individuals well-acquainted with the Siberian wilderness, this journey would ultimately prove to be their final adventure. Despite a thorough criminal investigation, the presence of photographs and journal entries, the Dyatlov Pass case remains unsolved even after more than fifty years have passed.

On January 23rd, 1959, a group of ten skiers and hikers boarded a train destined for the Ural Mountains in the heart of the Soviet Union. The group included eight men and two women, with Igor Dyatlov as their leader. As the train ventured deeper into the mountainous Siberian taiga, the group's diary received its last entry, pondering what awaited them on this excursion.

In the following days, the group switched between various modes of transportation, including a bus, a truck, a horse-drawn sleigh, and eventually proceeding on foot and skis. On January 28th, one of the hikers, Yuri Yudin, fell seriously ill and decided to return home, while the remaining nine members continued their planned journey. These photographs captured their last moments together, and it would be the final time Yuri saw his friends alive.

The group documented their expedition across the snow-covered wilderness, chronicling their experiences in diaries and through multiple cameras. Recovered photos and journal entries suggest that their trek progressed as expected, marked by snow, extreme cold, and a challenging landscape.

On February 1st, they reached the base of a mountain known to the indigenous Mansi population as Dead Mountain. After ascending the slope, they established a camp just a few hundred meters from the peak. Some of the last photos taken show a description of the harsh conditions they faced.

Several weeks passed without any communication from the group, causing concern among their friends and relatives. Eventually, a team of volunteers set out to find them. On February 26th, the search party finally located the camp on the slope. It became evident that something had gone horribly wrong. The tent was in disarray and covered by a light layer of snow. The group's belongings and equipment were neatly stored inside, but the tent had been slashed open from the inside with a knife.

The next day, nine sets of footprints led the search team downhill toward the nearby woods. The footprints did not indicate a panicked retreat, as they showed minimal indentation in the snow. They were followed for about half a kilometer until they vanished beneath the snow cover. Continuing in the direction of the tracks, the search party found the frozen bodies of Yuri Doroshenko and Yuri Krivonischenko under a large cedar tree near the remains of an improvised campfire.

It took over two months to recover the bodies of all nine hikers. The first two were found underdressed for the harsh climate, wearing only light shirts, underpants, and socks, despite temperatures around -30°C (-22°F). The cedar tree showed signs of damage, suggesting the possibility of the hikers attempting to locate the tent in the dark or trying to hide from something.

The next three hikers were found at varying distances from the tent and the tree, lightly dressed and lacking essential items. They all faced the direction of the tent at the time of their deaths, suggesting a struggle to return.

While some had minor injuries, all five died of hypothermia, with four of them having consumed alcohol before their deaths. The final four hikers were discovered at the bottom of a small hill, covered by 3 meters of snow, 75 meters from the tree, in the opposite direction of the tent. Three of them had suffered fatal injuries, with one having a fractured skull and two having multiple fractured ribs and internal bleeding. These injuries appeared to result from falls and were sustained while they were still alive. Two of the hikers were found with missing eyes, and one woman had a missing tongue. The last hiker had a broken nose and a deformed neck but died of hypothermia. Intriguingly, three articles of clothing were found to be abnormally radioactive.

On May 28th, the criminal case was abruptly closed with an enigmatic and vague conclusion. The lead investigator's final report stated, "The cause of death was an unknown compelling force which the hikers were unable to overcome." This left many questions unanswered and provided no satisfying explanation for the events. Therefore, in the absence of evidence linking the Galactic Empire to the incident, it remains a mystery with enigmatic details that demand a more specific yet credible explanation.

"Let's explore this in more detail. The significance of Dubinina's missing tongue has been somewhat exaggerated. Various theories have circulated regarding whether it was cut or torn while she was alive, devoured by scavengers post-mortem, or possibly found elsewhere. However, the medical reports provide a concise statement: 'The diaphragm of the mouth and the tongue are missing.' This statement lacks specifics about cutting or tearing. It's essential to note that this detail might have been deemed relatively minor by the medical examiner, as no elaboration was provided.

Similarly, the medical examiner addressed another mysterious aspect of the case—the 'gaping orbits' or missing eyeballs. The report attributes these findings to postmortem changes, specifically 'putrefaction and decomposition,' linked to Dubinina's corpse's exposure to water before discovery. This explanation clarifies the nature of the injuries.

One of the most perplexing elements of the case is the detection of radioactivity on three items of clothing worn by two of the hikers. Nevertheless, it's worth noting that radiation is relatively common in our environment. The radiological studies indicate that, under normal conditions, an area of 150 cm2 should not exceed 5000 disintegrations per minute (dpm). Only three articles of clothing registered values equal to or exceeding this limit, at 5000 dpm, 5600 dpm, and 9900 dpm. The report attributes this radioactivity to 'radioactive dust falling from the atmosphere' or potential contamination while in contact with radioactive substances. This suggests a possible natural source for the contamination, even if the exact cause remained undetermined.

However, an alternative explanation arises due to the backgrounds of two of the hikers, Kolevatov and Krivonischenko, who had prior involvement with nuclear materials. Kolevatov had worked at a facility developing nuclear materials, while Krivonischenko had experience at a top-secret plutonium production plant for nuclear weapons. Significantly, the three radioactive items of clothing belonged to Kolevatov and Krivonischenko.

Around the time of the hikers' disappearance, there were reported sightings of unidentified flying objects (UFOs), including orbs of light observed for varying durations in the night sky. Witnesses included three soldiers and two different hiking groups. Some individuals claimed that both the indigenous Mansi population and a group of geologists reported seeing fireballs in the sky during the same period. However, UFO sightings are often challenging to verify and identify, making them inconclusive as evidence.

Lastly, there's the enigmatic final photograph taken by one of the hikers. This photograph depicts a light source in the middle of the night. While it could indeed be a UFO, it could also be a photograph of a rocket, part of a rocket, space debris during reentry, a falling aircraft, or even a meteor. Given the era of the Cold War and the space race, there was substantial aerial activity. However, there's no clear link between the UFO sighting and the hikers' disappearance, making it a potential red herring.

So, what happened on that fateful night? Why did the hikers leave their tent, and why was the tent slashed from the inside? How did some hikers sustain severe injuries while others succumbed to the cold, and why were they underdressed? The biggest mystery is how this case has remained unsolved despite an abundance of information.

After an extensive investigation and careful consideration of various theories, one of the most credible explanations emerges. The key to understanding their actions lies in why they left the tent. It's plausible that an immediate threat within the tent prompted their exit. It is unlikely that an external threat, such as an animal or a UFO, would lead to the tent being cut open. Although there were no signs of an avalanche, they might have believed they were escaping one.

The calm and orderly footprints leading down the slope indicate that they composed themselves once outside the tent. Here's where the accidental reignition of the internal stove plays a pivotal role. After disassembling the stove and removing the exhaust pipe, the embers reignited, filling the tent with smoke. They cut holes in the tent's top to vent the smoke and eventually slashed the tent to escape the fumes, panicking in the process.

Additional evidence supporting this theory includes burn marks on their bodies and clothing, likely caused by the improvised fire under the tree or the hot stove. Some were found with blood around their mouths, suggesting smoke inhalation due to the tent's smoke.

They made a rushed exit, realizing their dire circumstances: sub-zero temperatures, inadequate clothing, a snowstorm, darkness, and isolation. In this desperate situation, one or more of them decided to seek refuge in the nearby woods. The smoke-filled tent could have made staying nearby impossible, or they may have believed the tent was on fire. Alcohol consumption might have clouded their judgment and sensitivity to the cold.

Reaching the woods, they attempted to start a fire. Some climbed the tree or scoured the area, while others ventured further into the woods. About 75 meters from the tree, four members triggered a minor avalanche, tumbling into a ravine with a 3-meter drop. Their injuries proved lethal, given the rocky and icy terrain at the ravine's base. Three others opted to return to the tent, while the remaining two succumbed to the cold, slowly freezing near their dwindling fire. This theory provides a comprehensive perspective on the events leading to the tragic outcome.

29. Vanishing Colony: The Mystery of Roanoke

Near the end of the 16th century, a man by the name of John White embarked on a transatlantic voyage. His destination was the island of Roanoke along the southeastern coast of North America. On this island, White had established an English colony some three years before, and he was now returning to resume his position as Governor. After a long and difficult journey, White finally reached the site of the colony only to find the more than one hundred men, women, and children he'd left behind had disappeared. A secret message carved into a tree was one of the only clues left behind at the scene. Before White had a chance to conduct a more extensive search, the ship returned to England, and in its wake, it left a mystery. What happened to the Lost Colony of Roanoke?

Before we can tackle the lost colony, we first need to understand the events leading up to its disappearance. The story begins in 1584 when two ships sailed across the Atlantic to scout for a suitable location for planting the first permanent English colony in America. In mid-July, they made landfall on a string of barrier islands known as the Outer Banks. The English quickly developed friendly relations with the local Native Americans and were soon invited to their village on Roanoke Island.

After about a month, the scouting expedition returned to their ships and sailed back to England. Upon the expedition's return in late September, the man in charge of the enterprise, Walter Raleigh, immediately began preparations to plant a permanent colony somewhere along the Outer Banks. Raleigh was soon thereafter knighted by Queen Elizabeth I, and the new land was to be named Virginia in honor of the Virgin Queen.

In April of 1585, a fleet of seven ships departed England with a complement of roughly 600 men and loaded with enough provisions to sustain the colony for about a year. The fleet reached the Outer Banks at the end of June but was soon faced with a crisis. Navigating the waters of the Outer Banks can be notoriously treacherous, as indicated by these sinking ships, and when the flagship passed through one of the shallow inlets, it struck a shoal and was nearly destroyed. As the flagship carried the bulk of the provisions and most of it was now spoiled by seawater, the scope of the colony had to be dramatically reduced. About 100 men, far fewer than initially intended, were stationed on Roanoke Island, and, with the natives' approval, they began construction of what was to become the Roanoke colony.

The island was primarily chosen for its strategic value. It provided quick access to the ocean while still making the colony invisible to Spanish patrols. Spain had already colonized and laid claim to much of what the English now called Virginia, so they had to be careful not to attract any unwanted attention. A second wave of supplies and reinforcements was expected to arrive before the winter, but, unbeknownst to the colonists, the resupply mission had been countermanded by the Queen to deal with more pressing concerns back in England. As such, once the colonists ran out of food, they had to rely on the generosity of the natives. However, the natives only had so much to spare and struggled to meet the increasing demands by the colonists. This overdependence quickly began to strain their relationship.

Meanwhile, people had begun to notice a disturbing trend. Every time the English visited a Native American village, many of its inhabitants would inexplicably collapse and die. The natives believed the English could kill from a distance by shooting invisible bullets, and they were not too far off. While unknown at the time, the English were carrying deadly pathogens to which the natives lacked immunity, and thus an epidemic was unwittingly unleashed upon the indigenous population.

The two leaders back on Roanoke, colonial governor Ralph Lane and Indian chieftain Wingina, eventually grew so suspicious of one another that cohabitation was no longer possible. Wingina decided to remove his people from the island and retreated to a larger village on the mainland. Meanwhile, Lane came to believe that Wingina had formed an alliance with other tribes and that they were plotting to launch an attack against the colony. Whether he was paranoid or not, Lane decided to take preemptive action.

On June 1, 1586, Lane and his men made their way to the mainland village and massacred its people. One of the Englishmen chased after and decapitated Wingina, and his head was later impaled outside the fort of the colony. A week later, a large English fleet, commanded by the renowned sea captain Sir Francis Drake, dropped by the Outer Banks on its way back to England. Given the lack of food and violent clashes with the natives, it was decided to abandon the colony. The colonists were hastily evacuated off the island, and then, after nine long months, they all returned home. All, except three, who were not located in time for the evacuation, and so the fleet left them behind. They were never heard from again.

If the scouting expedition of 1584 had been a resounding success, the colony of 1585 was a categorical failure. Relations with the Native Americans had completely fallen apart, the severe lack of food had made life miserable, and they had failed to track down rumored sources of gold and copper, which could have made the venture worthwhile. In spite of all this, at least one man was eager to return. His name was John White. White was a painter and artist by trade, and many of the maps and sketches that you've seen so far were either drawn by him or based on his work. Somewhat ironically, however, there are no surviving portraits of White himself.

White's participation in these earlier voyages is slightly ambiguous. He may have been part of the scouting expedition in 1584, but he was definitely part of the voyage in '85. What is a bit unclear is whether he stayed behind at the colony or returned to England with the outbound fleet. For instance, White's name is not included in a surviving list of all the colonists. But some historians believe this is merely an oversight and that he was, in fact, part of the colony. In either case, Sir Walter Raleigh was eventually persuaded by White and others to attempt a second venture. Unlike the first colony, which had been more akin to a military outpost, the second would include women and children, including White's pregnant daughter, Elenore

Dare. After a long struggle to secure the necessary funding, a fleet of three ships, commanded by White, who would also serve as Governor of the colony, departed England in late spring of 1587.

The misfortune of the first colony did not end with its evacuation in 1586. Only days later, a ship filled with provisions, sent by Sir Walter Raleigh, arrived at the Outer Banks. The crew spent some time searching for the colonists, but when they found no sign of them, including the three men that had been left behind, they returned home. The same thing happened two weeks later when an English-bound fleet, loaded with supplies and reinforcements, also found the colony deserted. Unwilling to leave the colony vacant, however, the Captain left 15 crewmen on Roanoke before the fleet resumed the course for England.

John White had been told about the 15 crewmen before he departed, so when his fleet

approached the Outer Banks in late July of 1587, he intended to pay them a visit. But this is where things get confusing. You see, the second colony was never intended to be established on Roanoke. After all, the long list of complications encountered by the first colony made it clear that Roanoke was far from an ideal location. Instead, the second colony, or the Cittie of Raleigh as the man in charge had so immodestly named it, was to be planted somewhere along the coast of Chesapeake Bay. This made a lot more sense. The water was deeper to allow for larger ships, and not nearly as precarious as those around the Outer Banks. There was plenty of open space. The soil was more fertile, and, all around, it seemed an improvement to Roanoke Island.

But the fleet's Portuguese navigator, Simão Fernandes, had other plans. Fernandes had also been the navigator of the two previous expeditions and was a far more experienced sailor than White. So even though White was officially the Captain, it seems much of the crew respected the authority of Fernandes. As such, when Fernandes decided to ignore the plan about Chesapeake Bay and, instead, simply dump the colonists on Roanoke, White did nothing to challenge his decision. The rest of the crew quickly fell in line, and, soon enough, everyone disembarked for Roanoke.

Upon reaching the abandoned colony, there was no sign of the 15 crewmen they had come to assist. Instead, they found a pile of bones that appeared to be the remains of one of them. White suspected the men had been attacked by vengeful Indians, and any doubts he might have had were soon to be erased. After only a few days on the island, a colonist by the name of George Howe was attacked by a group of natives who pelted him with 16 arrows before caving in his skull with a wooden club. A brutal yet unmistakable message. The English were no longer welcome on Roanoke.

Even so, the colonists were not without allies. You see, when the scouting expedition returned to England in 1584, two Native Americans, named Wanchese and Manteo, were brought along with them. Wanchese was from Roanoke, while Manteo was from a neighboring village on the island of Croatoan. When they were finally brought back to North America in 1585, they had developed vastly different opinions of the English people.

As soon as they made landfall, Wanchese returned to Roanoke with nothing but resentment for these foreign invaders. Meanwhile, Manteo was fascinated by everything the English had to offer. He became their trusted guide and a mediator of sorts to smooth out relations upon first contact. So, following the death of George Howe, White reached out to the Croatoans, and they confirmed what he'd initially suspected. A large group of Indian tribes had indeed attacked the 15 crewman station on Roanoke. This coalition was spearheaded by none other than Wanchese. At least two of the crewmen had been killed in the attack, while the rest escaped in a small boat, never to be seen again. Roanoke had become a much more dangerous place to live.

Simão Fernandes remained anchored near the Outer Banks for about a month before he decided to return to England. In the meantime, the colonists had grown concerned about the long-term survival of the colony. If the colony were to be truly self-sufficient, they argued they would require more people and more food. As such, they implored Governor White to return to England with Fernandes so that he could bring back supplies and restock the colony.

White was initially hesitant to leave as he feared he'd be accused of desertion if he returned to England alone. Not to mention, he would have to abandon his daughter, who had recently given birth to a daughter of her own, named Virginia, on this remote and precarious island. But, in time, he was persuaded to go. And as the fleet departed in late August of 1587, he could not have known he would never see any of them again.

After a long and difficult voyage, John White returned to a country at war. By orders of the Queen, no ships were to leave England until the threat of Spanish invasion had passed. This was bad news for White, and his best efforts notwithstanding, he remained trapped in England for three long years. It was not until the spring of 1590, with the help of Sir Walter Raleigh, that White finally managed to book passage on a convoy bound for America.

Upon reaching the Outer Banks in mid-August, plumes of smoke appeared to emanate from Roanoke Island. Two boats were quickly dispatched, and the crew fired the ship's cannons to make their presence known. The men could see a great fire as they approached the island, but White never clarifies whether it was natural or lit by people. Once ashore, they made their way to the west end of the island and found a set of footprints. They appeared to be fresh, but there was no sign of those to whom they belonged.

The search party then headed north and happened upon a tree where someone had carved the letters C-R-O. Upon reaching the entrance of the colony, they came across a second inscription. It was the word CROATOAN, engraved into a wooden post. The post was but one of many that now formed a defensive barrier around the colony. The colony itself was deserted and clearly had been for some time, given the overgrowth of grass and weeds. The houses had been taken down and stripped of valuables. All they found were bars of iron, a few cannons, as well as five looted chests. There was no trace of the roughly 115 colonists nor the small boats left in their possession. As far as anyone could tell, no one had lived here for quite some time.

The story of the Lost Colony is often centered around the two engravings, and without the full context, it's easy to see how an author might imbue these inscriptions with intrigue and mystery. In truth, the carvings are some of the more well-understood elements of the entire story. At least, John White had no doubts about their meaning.

White explains in his notes that before he left in 1587, he and the colonists had come to an agreement. If they decided to abandon the colony before the Governor's return, they were to leave behind a secret token of their destination. Furthermore, if this abandonment was forced upon them, they were to include a cross to signify distress. Because no such cross had been found, White was confident the colonists had safely relocated to the island of Croatoan.

Thus, White swiftly returned to the ship and convinced the Captain to set course for Croatoan. But while the crew prepared for departure, the anchor cable snapped. And without a spare anchor, the Captain felt it was too dangerous to continue. In the end, White never made it to Croatoan, and it was the last time he ever ventured across the Atlantic.

Twenty years after the Roanoke colony was lost, the Anglo-Spanish war had come to an end. John White faded into obscurity, and Sir Walter Raleigh had been found guilty of treason for conspiring against the crown. Yeah, I know, it's a whole other thing. Anyway, renewed interest in America saw the plantation of a third colony in 1607. The Jamestown colony was established within the borders of a vast confederacy of Native American tribes ruled by a man the English called Powhatan.

One day, Powhatan captured the future Governor of the colony, John Smith, and told him about a place where men wearing European clothing lived. Then, after his release in 1608, Smith drew a rough map of Virginia, and this is one of the notations. Unfortunately, this claim, and others just like it, were never properly investigated. So we can never know if this was anything more than a rumor. Another unconfirmed report was that all but a few of the colonists had been massacred by Powhatan. The survivors of this slaughter at Roanoke had then supposedly scattered across the region. The problem is, White did not report any human remains or signs of a battle when he returned to Roanoke in 1590.

Even so, an acquaintance of John Smith later wrote that Powhatan had confessed to the massacre after Smith was captured. Smith himself, however, makes no mentioned of this alleged confession, and he was not exactly known to shy away from embellishment. *cough* Pocahontas *cough* Other reports included sightings of Native American children with unusually pale skin and blonde hair, which led many to suspect they could be the descendants of the lost colonists. What they had no way of knowing at the time, however, was that albinism is far more prevalent among Native Americans than Europeans.

A more solid lead emerged a full century later when the English explorer John Lawson made contact with a tribe known as the Hatteras. The Hatteras occupied the same land as the Croatoans, but the island was now much larger and known as Hatteras Island after a storm had closed one of the inlets. The Hatteras explained to Lawson that some of their ancestors had been white and able to read. Several members of the tribe also had gray eyes, a unique trait of the Hatteras, according to Lawson. They also spoke of a local legend about a ghost ship, which they referred to as Sir Walter Raleigh's ship.

Hearing all this, Lawson grew convinced the Hatteras was, in fact, the descendants of the lost colony. Much like John White, Lawson believed the colony had been relocated to Croatoan, and, over time, the two peoples had become one. Okay, so we now have two sources, over a century apart, arguing for the same version of events. John White says they went to Croatoan because carvings. John Lawson says they went to Croatoan because gray eyes and ghosts. Not the most decisive evidence, perhaps, but it does make for a compelling argument.

Following Lawson's encounter with the Hatteras in 1701, nothing of significance would be uncovered for centuries. That is until the late 1930s when a series of peculiar stones suddenly brought the mystery back to life. The stones had been inscribed with messages, supposedly written by Elenore Dare, the daughter of John White. Unfortunately, they all turned out to be fake. Well, all except the first stone whose authenticity remains in doubt.

This stone features a message from Dare addressed to White in which she describes the tragic death of her husband and child. The composition of the stone makes it well-suited for inscribing a message but a poor choice for a forger as they would have had to chemically age the fresh markings to match the weathered surface. It would not have been impossible but quite difficult to do so in the 1930s. On the other hand, the man who supposedly found the stone was never heard from again, and the precise location of its discovery was conveniently kept secret. The credibility of the writing is equally contested, and there is just no consensus on what to make of it.

Modern archaeological research has also been plagued by uncertainties. Excavations at Roanoke have mostly confirmed the presence of a 16th-century English colony but have done little in the way of determining its fate. Meanwhile, excavations on Hatteras have yielded a mix of Native American and European artifacts, including the hilt of a light sword, but nothing that can be definitively linked to the lost colony. To make matters worse, much of the evidence may now be underwater due to centuries of shifting sands and erosion of the islands.

It was partially out of frustration for this lack of progress that researchers made a remarkable discovery in late 2011. While inspecting White's map of Virginia, a member of the First Colony Foundation took note of these patches. Historically, patches like these have been used to correct minor mistakes, so no one had ever given them a second thought. This time, someone did and had the patches carefully examined. Underneath the lower patch, they found precisely what you'd expect. Minor corrections. Underneath to upper patch, however, they found this.

This four-pointed star is a typical representation of a fort. A comparable symbol can be seen on this map from the early 17th century. The paint used to draw the symbol matches the paint used elsewhere on the map, including the corrections drawn on top of the lower patch, suggesting it was drawn and concealed by White himself. More puzzling still... A slightly smaller four-pointed star enclosed by two concentric squares has been painted with invisible ink on top of the patch. This symbol can even be faintly discerned with the naked eye, meaning it's been hiding in plain sight all along.

Finally, this fort is situated on the mainland, approximately 50 miles west of Roanoke.

The location of the concealed fort was quickly named Site X in reference to the X-shaped symbol. Its discovery was followed by a search for the remains of this fort, which, if it had been built by the lost colonists, could potentially hold the key to the colony's fate. Before long, excavations began at Site X. The work did not yield a fort, but it did turn up English artifacts from the 16th century, though nothing that could be definitively linked to the colony. Furthermore, artifacts that were discovered had been heavily disturbed, making it difficult to assess their age.

Overall, the 2012 excavation was a disappointment, and the team quickly found themselves in the same position as countless others who had come before. And, even worse, the sheer abundance of artifacts at the site made it clear that it was inhabited by people long after the colonists had been lost. Ultimately, the researchers decided to abandon Site X for the time being and focus their attention on a neighboring area where they'd previously unearthed a number of intriguing artifacts.

In 2013, a team of archaeologists began excavations in this new area, which they called Coree, after the Coree Indians who once lived in the vicinity. Much to their excitement, they quickly uncovered what appeared to be an early colonial site. But the ruins did not match those of the Roanoke colony. Rather, it more closely resembled a military outpost. Its peculiar star-shaped design, for instance, was reminiscent of a fort from the same era in Ireland. One of the first artifacts to be found was a copper token from a political prisoner in England, which further supported the idea that the site had once served as a military post.

As work on the site continued, more and more artifacts began to emerge. Among them was a piece of window lead, the kind used in early 17th-century England. While intriguing, it could not definitively be linked to the site's date of construction. As they continued to dig, the archaeologists unearthed a number of early 17th-century pottery fragments, again confirming the site's construction during this time period.

Most importantly, perhaps, was the discovery of a hearth that had likely been used to fire muskets, something which suggested it could have been a military fort after all. But when the researchers finally reached the fort's ditch, or moat, they found the crucial evidence they'd been searching for. In a layer of dirt dating from the late 16th century, they discovered a number of early colonial artifacts, such as gunflints and pottery fragments.

And then, lying on the bottom of the moat, one of the archaeologists found this. It's the iron barrel of a type of heavy weapon known as a breech-loading swivel gun. And it was this artifact, in particular, that led the researchers to believe they had uncovered the remains of the lost colony's military outpost. In case it's not clear, this would be a big deal. While it's still not clear what happened to the Roanoke colonists, the artifacts from the Coree site make it clear they were in this vicinity for some time before they were lost. This is far more than we can say for most previous excavations. For this reason, most have come to accept the Coree site as one of the best candidates for finding answers to the mystery.

Some have taken this to the next logical step, and by examining artifacts that were in use by the late 16th century, they hope to piece together the story of the colony itself. Others have set their sights on the thousands of Native American artifacts that have been recovered over the years. Given that the colony did have substantial contact with the local population, an analysis of these artifacts might finally reveal what happened to the colonists. So, even though the lost colony is no longer entirely lost, its story remains incomplete. As such, the secret of Roanoke is likely to keep historians and archaeologists busy for years to come.

In the end, the Lost Colony of Roanoke remains one of the great unsolved mysteries of American history. Despite the efforts of countless researchers and the discovery of new evidence, we are left with more questions than answers. What happened to the people of Roanoke? Did they assimilate with Native American tribes, as some theories suggest? Were they killed by hostile natives or attacked by the Spanish, who had a presence in the region? Did they try to return to England in their small boats and become lost at sea? The truth may never be known, and the mystery of the Lost Colony of Roanoke will likely continue to intrigue and perplex for generations to come.